Go Live Life

Conquering Fear, Anxiety & Overthinking

Tony Haygood

Go Live Life
Conquering Fear, Anxiety and Overthinking
ISBN: 979-8-9881994-2-7
© 2024 by Tony Haygood

Text Design: Lisa Simpson

Contents

Dedication

To my beautiful wife, Miriam. You have not lived a life of fear but rather spent your life helping me with mine. I owe you my life. You are the true definition of fearlessness.

Acknowledgements

This book was a joy to write! I really feel like God helped me express what was inside, finally getting it onto the printed page. I am thankful. Still, work like this took many people and much time. I sincerely want to show gratitude to those who made this possible.

Lisa Carrillo, your friendship means so much to me. Your encouraging words have helped me during some of my darkest days. You have always shown such kindness to me and my family, and I will forever be grateful for the lifetime of friendship we have shared. I truly value your inner strength, your gentle smile, and the integrity you hold in your heart. You are a true Jesus follower. Thank you!

Renae Cockroft, I don't know how you put up with me and my sloppy writing, but I am so thankful that you have. Once again, your editing talents, suggestions, and commitment to help me have pulled things together to completion. I am truly thankful for you and your friendship.

Lisa Simpson, thank you for taking words and turning them into art. You have a gift that I do not. I believe that your contribution to this book will help countless lives find freedom. Thank you for utilizing your skills to make this book a reality.

And, to my wife, Miriam. Thank you for helping me find my way. Your life inspires me to do better, to learn more, and to put God first. You have faced fear with more courage than me, stayed more balanced than me, and displayed more grace than me in the process. I feel like you could have written this book in a fraction of the time! I love you so much!

Foreword

I would like to take a moment to share with you an incredible book that has had a profound impact on my life. "Go Live Life" by Tony Haygood is a must-read for anyone who has ever felt held back by fear. As someone who has known Tony for over thirty years, I can attest to his loving nature, dedicated ministry, and unwavering friendship. This book reflects his character, filled with inspiring stories and real-life examples that shine a light on the darkness of fear. It offers simple yet powerful keys to unlock the chains of fear and live a life full of freedom. Through reading "Go Live Life," I have identified areas in my own life where fear had control. However, Tony's words helped me gain a greater awareness of how to overcome those fears and walk in freedom. I am convinced that anyone who reads this book will benefit from the revelation and freedom it offers. If you've ever struggled with fear or anxiety, I highly recommend that you read "Go Live Life." Tony asks the thought-provoking question, "How long will you wait to be free?" I encourage you to take that first step towards freedom today. Don't let fear hold you back any longer. Trust me; this book will change your life.

Lisa Carrillo

Preface

I suppose I have been pretty fearful for the majority of my life. It seems like I was constantly surrounded by different uncertainties, challenges, and crazy circumstances, and as a result, I let fear find its way into my heart and mind. Fear was paralyzing me, hindering me, and stealing from me the abundant life God intended for me to have. But I eventually found out that fear did not have to be my constant companion. We all can rise above it, conquer it, and experience true freedom in our lives.

I am not pretending to know everything about fear, but I can tell you that I have lived through some pretty terrible things in my life, most of which were self-imposed. There have been times when I let fear and worry haunt me and hold me back. I remember very well how that felt to me, and I would never want that for anyone else. There were times that fear completely stopped me in my tracks and prevented me from moving forward.

My intention in writing this book is to expose some of those fears and to show you what you can do to overcome fear, worry, and anxiety in your life. I have written this book from a Christian point of view and purposely utilized Bible scriptures throughout to help overcome these fears. If you can understand the kind of worry or fear that you are dealing with and if you can accurately see where it leads, you can then arm yourself with the proper information to overcome any fear, worry, or dread you may face.

I think it is funny that certain people in life just seem to be "happy-go-lucky." They do not seem to have a care in the world. Nothing really seems to bother them. My wife is one of those people. We could not be more opposite in that way. Those kinds of people do not seem to have as many problems with fear as others do. One person can stand right at the edge of a tall building on the 40th floor without any consideration of the possibility of falling to their death, while another person shrinks back and has a tight grip on the handrail, just to make absolutely sure there is no chance they will make it close to the edge. One person can happily quit their job and venture out into the unknown, ready to try something new, just excited to see what the future holds, not even knowing where the next paycheck will come from. And yet someone else will go through the painstaking task of pre-calculating every possible scenario, considering all the options for months or years, just to try not to get behind financially, lose their home, and fall into financial ruin. One person seems to be able to throw caution to the wind and jump out of a perfectly working airplane to participate in the thrill of a parachute jump that has them descending toward the Earth at a high rate of speed, only to open their chute at the last moment, completely enjoying the exhilarating ride of their life. At the same time, the next person seems perfectly content to stay on the ground and video the entire event from the safety of their vehicle. Two different people with two very different directions and outcomes. I think that is amazing! By the way, I was the second person! People are so different. They say things differently. They think differently. Some people seem predisposed to not worry or take on the burden of caring too much at all, while others seem to care about everything in the world.

This book is written from the perspective of someone who has walked around with fear most of his life and knows the sensations and feelings of terror that come with it very well. Someone who knows the devastation that fear, anxiety, and worry can cause in your everyday life. It is also co-authored by someone who has experienced much freedom from those fears and has an eye to a bright future that is free from anxiety. In this case, both authors just happen to be the same person — me! I do understand that this book may not be for everyone. If you are in a group that takes life one day at a time and has no issue with fear, thank you for taking the time to pick this book up; you are now dismissed. Feel free to embark on your next dangerous mission! You are probably already planning your next base jump adventure or scuba dive in shark-infested waters right now! I genuinely hope you have a great time, and I wish you all the best. If, on the other hand, you are in a group that constantly battles with fear, anxiety, and worry, this is the book for you! It will not be too difficult to spot you, as you will be clinging firmly to the handrail at a safe distance from the edge!

Throughout these pages, we will delve into the depths of various fears that have plagued humanity for far too long — the fear of man, fear of failure, fear of lack, fear of change, and so many more. We will uncover their roots, explore their devastating effects, and discover the tools and principles necessary to overcome them. You will find a wealth of scriptural references, personal stories, and practical exercises that will guide you toward your own personal freedom from fear. This is simply a collection of wisdom, insights, practical strategies, and biblical truths that will equip and empower you to break free from the grip of fear. Trust me, life is a lot better after fear!

Fifteen of the chapters in this book are dedicated to addressing very specific fears that many individuals face. I will provide guidance and encouragement on how to conquer those fears and experience lasting transformation. I understand that it could be very tempting to just jump ahead to the chapters that you might need help with, but I want to strongly discourage you from doing that. I believe that you need to be armed with the information leading up to those chapters in order for them to have the greatest meaning and impact for you. I do not want you to miss any of the information that could help you on your journey to overcome fear once and for all. These chapters are not merely intellectual exercises. They are born out of real-life experiences, personal triumphs, and the understanding that God desires us to live fearlessly in this life, holding His hand all the way through. You will be encouraged to face your fears head-on, holding onto the truth that you are not alone. God is with you, and His perfect love casts out fear. We will talk about that in detail a little later.

After I graduated high school in Florida, I found myself moving out to Texas to attend Bible college. Those were good days of intense study in the Word of God, and I honestly enjoyed every moment of it. I decided to also go to work for a ministry in Texas and ended up working there for almost 35 years. I never dreamed I would stay in the same place that long, but that is exactly what happened. The problem was that over a period of many years, I also allowed fear to creep into my life in various ways. I handed over many of my freedoms voluntarily due to the imagination I had built in my mind. I allowed my job to take over my life and keep me from the family time that should have been my priority. The fear that I accepted into my heart and mind kept me from stepping out and doing the things I needed to do. It was no one's fault but my own. I chose it. I agreed to it. I allowed it. Looking back on those days, I realize that I probably needed to change my career path about a decade sooner than I did, but I was bound by fear. The fear I experienced led me to believe that my life would fall into chaos if I left that job. After all, how would I go about feeding my family and keeping my kids in a good school? How would I begin a whole new career at my age? How would I be financially supported and provide for my family? So many questions. So many *fearful* questions that kept me from stepping out. In my case, I had to have outside help come along in the form of another pastor and a very close life-long friend. Together, these two men spoke into my life things that I needed to hear. I had many meetings and conversations with these men that ended up resulting in my freedom from fear. They continuously prayed with me and spoke the Word of God to me, which ultimately built confidence in me and allowed me to move forward. I remember very well the day that I was praying about turning in my resignation after nearly 35 years. I wanted to check with God one more time to make sure that I was making the right decision. It was a big, life-changing move. Once I turned in that resignation, I would be stepping into the wide world of nothingness. I had no future job lined up. I would simply be stepping out, trusting God Almighty that He would make a way for me where there seemed to be no way. I got in my car that day and just drove and drove. I was praying, I was crying, and I was pouring my heart out to God. I needed that final piece of assurance from God that this was the right thing to do.

God answered me that day with three very simple words. Those words were, "Go Live Life!" As soon as I heard them, I knew I had the answer I needed. Those three little words changed my life completely. I had the reassurance in my heart that things were going to work out. At that point, it was just a matter of turning in my resignation and talking to the people that I had worked for all those years. It was not easy to leave people that I knew so well and loved so much, but it was time. It was a few days later that I was able to hand in my resignation. As soon as I did, and that paper left my hand, I experienced a true freedom from fear and a supernatural peace from God Almighty that remains with me to this day. I am so thankful that God gave me that peace and assurance. By the way, everything turned out fine, and I ended up with nearly a year off. God provided every step of the way, and every bill that needed to be paid was paid. We found good schools for our children. We did not lose our house or vehicles. In fact, we ended up doing about 20% better financially during that time than we had at any other time in our lives. And now, you know the reason for the title of this book. You see, those three simple words represent freedom from fear, and that is what this book is all about.

The journey toward freedom from fear is not always easy, but it is worth every step. As you open this book, I encourage you to open your heart, too! Open yourself to the transforming power of God's Word. Allow God's powerful words to penetrate deep inside you, challenging your beliefs and your mindset.

This book is not a quick fix for your life or a magic formula for instant freedom. It is an invitation to embark on a journey of growth, faith, and personal transformation. It is all about discovering the depths of God's love and the abundance of His promises. I hope you will take the time to get all you can from this information.

I remember a time, one morning, when I walked into the kitchen area of our house only to find my young son, Joshua, there already eating a bowl of cereal. He must have been about five or six years old at the time. Normally, this would not have been unusual, but today it was. I looked up at my son sitting at the table, and in his right hand, he had two spoons. Two spoons in one hand, side-by-side. In essence, he had put the two spoons together to make a much wider spoon. I remember asking him that morning, "Joshua, why are you using two spoons to eat your cereal?" He replied, "Dad, I just wanted to get all I could get!" Children say the funniest things! So, as you read through this material, I encourage you to do what my son did and "get all you can get!" Take time to reflect on the scriptures and allow the Holy Spirit to speak to you in the depths of your soul. Sometimes, it may be best to read for a while and then go back and reread that same section again. The idea here is not to rush through the pages looking for a quick pill to take that will make everything better, but rather to really let God's Word be an encouragement to you and a reminder that fear does not define you, and it does not have the final say in your life. In this case, the actual journey of overcoming fear is just as important as the destination of the freedom it brings. You were created for a purpose, and God has equipped you with everything you need to overcome fear and live a life marked by faith, courage, and joy.

"For God gave us a spirit
not of fear but of power and love
and self-control." (2 Timothy 1:7, ESV)

I hope that as you read through these pages, you will ultimately conclude that it is time to be free from fear and **Go Live Life.**

"The greatest mistake we make is living in
constant fear that we will make one."
—John C. Maxwell

1

Why is Fear
Such a Big Deal?

Have you ever heard someone say, "I have some good news and some bad news?" If that question was posed to you, which news would you typically pick first to receive? Did you know that multiple studies over a long period of time have shown that roughly four out of five people prefer to begin with the bad news? They would much rather start with a loss or negative information and ultimately end with a gain or positive outcome rather than the reverse. It ends up being around 78% of the time. There are currently many different TED Talks on this very subject. We would like to finish on a good note! Have you ever eaten a nice meal and saved that one last little bite just because you knew it would leave a good taste in your mouth when you were finished? I know I have! I think oftentimes it is because we want to be left with something positive, we want to end up with the good news, and we want to walk away with a good taste in our mouth. Well, I have some good news for you, and I have some bad news for you! Which would you like to hear first? Okay, we will start with the bad news! Fear is horrible! Fear is just terrible!

The reason that fear is such a big deal is that it is a debilitating thing. Fear is unhealthy because it makes you more cautious than you need to be to stay safe and prevents you from doing things you would otherwise enjoy. Fear is absolutely terrible. Fear will haunt you. It will hold you back. It will keep you from accomplishing your goals. Fear will stop you in your tracks. It will prevent your progress and diminish your life entirely. Fear is a crushing thing. It is a terrifying thing. And the worst part is that you were never supposed to be in fear at all, and yet here we are.

Fear is known by many different names. The dictionary defines fear as an unpleasant emotion caused by the belief that someone or something is dangerous and likely to cause pain or a threat. But fear seems to always take things too far. When fear starts talking, it makes the stakes a lot higher. So, instead of thinking that something bad is just "possibly" going to happen, it turns it into something bad that is "most likely" going to happen or "will" happen! Do you see the difference? Fear likes to always move in the direction of certainty that bad will happen. Fear and exaggeration go hand-in-hand!

You see, worry is temporary. Worry gets you to use problem-solving skills to address your concerns. But anxiety is persistent, even when concerns are unrealistic. It often compromises your ability to function. Fear is a feeling of anxiety concerning the outcome of something. It is the likelihood of something unwelcome happening. It is to dread something that is coming. Does any of that sound familiar? You must also understand that worry, anxiety, depression, dread, and overthinking all seem to run together. They are very close friends. When you find one of these, you need to understand that the others are probably lingering close by. So, throughout this book, we will continue to discuss each of these things and even use them interchangeably at times because they all have their root in fear. Although these things might be slightly different in their definition, ultimately, entertaining any of these things will lead to failure and destruction. None of these things will ever work in your favor. It is important to understand how these things attempt to operate in your life and what to do about it when they try. Remember, I am giving you the bad news first!

Fear and anxiety tend to grip people who are more structurally organized. People who tend to think a lot. Did you ever notice that? People who are deep thinkers. Type A personalities. This happens to describe me perfectly! I fit in this category quite nicely. This happens because we tend to overthink every situation. We worry a lot. Overthinkers tend to be predisposed to worry and fear. But we can reverse this cycle. The Bible has a lot to say about fear and worry.

To worry is to decide in advance that you have lost without having any evidence to prove it. Fear robs you of your future by predetermining your failure. Anxiety does not ever provide a "plan B" for success but can only see the doom in the current situation. I know; I lived this way for many, many years.

One of the main reasons that I decided to write this book is because I struggled with this so much myself. I used to really think that I had everything together. I used to think that I had everything under control and that fear really was not a reality in my life. After all, I was a fine Christian young man, working at a church, ministering to other people, and even teaching the Bible. I did not really have any problems in those areas, but behind the scenes, I was riddled with fear. I walked in a constant fear of man. I lacked the ability to break free from this on my own and ultimately had to have outside help. There were changes that I desperately needed to make in my life that would benefit my family and me, but because of the overwhelming fear at work in my life, I just could not bring myself to make the changes. It was horrible. You see, I thought I had all my ducks in a row, but I will tell you that was far from the truth. For quite a while, I had no idea how much fear I was operating in on a daily basis. For me, fear kept me tied down, indecisive, frozen in my tracks, and without the real ability to change.

To worry is to decide in advance that you have lost without having any evidence to prove it.

Worry, fear, and dread will ruin your dreams, and count them as impossible before you ever take the first step to accomplish them. **It is like giving up before you ever start, based solely on false information that only exists in your mind.** It is self-deception. We do this to ourselves because we see fear as bigger than success and bigger than God. Ultimately, fear holds you back from achieving the success you deserve through God.

We must learn to rid our lives of fear. We must seek it out in every dark corner of our lives and eradicate it. Nothing positive ever comes from fear. Fear has torment attached to it. The Bible says that in 1 John 4:18. We must learn to stop living with anxiety, coping with worry, subjecting ourselves to fear, and pretending to have none. It is time to look fear directly in the face and overcome it once and for all. It is time to step into new areas, step out in faith, face our fears, and overcome them.

I want to be clear that throughout this book, as we continue to discuss fear, anxiety, and worry, I will also present the good along with the bad. I will discuss the horrible part of fear, quickly followed by some solutions for that particular kind of fear. I will specifically be doing this because I do not want you to have to read very far to find some hope in your situation. I literally do not want you to worry about reading too far without an answer. You might think I am kidding here, but I promise you, I am not. If you are the kind of person who has walked in fear for any part of your life, you will understand what I just said and greatly appreciate having a positive answer close by rather than waiting to get to the end of the book to get the answers. Some of you might worry that this book does not contain the answers. Just hold on; we are going to get there together!

One of the ways that fear can occupy your life is by false assumptions. For many, many years, I struggled with a broken "assumer!" Let me explain. Each of us has an assumer built into the inside of us. It is the place deep inside us where we assume things. One of the negative results of allowing fear and worry into your life is that it will also break your assumer. Let me give you an example. When your assumer is broken, in your mind, you will preemptively assume that you will not have enough money to get something done, that you will not have enough time to get it done, that it will be too hard for you to get it done, that it will take too long for you to get it done, and ultimately decide that it is just not worth even starting! When your assumer is broken, you constantly assume the worst-case scenario. Believe me, I know! If you doubt me for a second, ask my wife, and she will let you know how much I have struggled with this. With a broken assumer, it is nearly impossible to see any perspective other than failure and doom. It is a complete mind game. It is a very difficult thing to deal with. It is also extremely difficult for people who do not struggle with a broken assumer to ever understand those who do. However, when you finally get your assumer fixed, many things start to automatically make sense. Suddenly, you flip that switch on the inside of you, and now you are able to preemptively assume that you will have enough money and time to get something done. You now assume that it won't be too hard for you or take too long for you to get it done, and ultimately, you will decide that it is absolutely worth starting and pursuing. What a difference! What a difference it will make in your life to move from a place of having a broken assumer to having a fixed assumer. This made all the difference in the world for me personally.

In my case, my assumer was so broken by fear and worry that I had to have outside help to finally get it fixed! That's right, I said that I had to have someone else come along with me and help me understand what it would take to finally fix my assumer so I could get back on track and live life. Sometimes, you must have additional outside help to overcome certain things. Sometimes, you need someone to help you see things from a different perspective. This is precisely what my friend Mark Carrillo did for me as my life coach. Even though my own family had attempted to help me with these things for many years, I still could not see it. My wife tried, my children tried, but for me, it still took an outside perspective to get my attention.

I remember a time many years ago when I was a boy at summer camp. Since I was born and raised in Florida, summer camps were always hot and humid. I never really cared for it myself. During the camp times, there were always a lot of activities for everyone to do, and inevitably, one of them was a giant tug-of-war contest. I remember very vividly doing this one year at camp. There must have been about 20 people on each side. I remember that day very well because it was also raining and very muddy. So, there we were out in the middle of the camp in a big muddy area while it was raining, about to begin the tug-of-war game. Everything was evenly matched, with one exception: one of our teammates had to go to the restroom at the last minute and just left us there without him. No one seemed to notice that he had left, so the game started without him. Well, you can probably imagine how this went! We were down a man. We were in trouble! We were really struggling because the sides were not evenly matched. We were giving it all that we had, but our feet were just sliding in the mud, and we were getting closer and closer to defeat. Then, suddenly, that same guy came bursting back on the scene, grabbed the rope, and started pulling. He was a big guy, too! We ended up winning the contest that day, but it was only because we had the additional help that we needed to get the job done. That is what I am trying to say. Sometimes, you just need someone else pulling for you to win the game. I would like to be that someone for you!

Ultimately, only Jesus can help any of us overcome and keep fear out of our lives. The Bible says that perfect love casts out fear, and Jesus is perfect love. We were never designed to be fearful creatures. We were not intended to carry weights, tensions, burdens, or fears. All these things come under the category of "the cares of this life." And the Bible is clear that we are supposed to cast our cares on the Lord because He cares for us. We were never strong enough to carry our own cares, but Jesus is ready to take them for us.

It is up to us to renew our minds to the things of God, looking at and meditating on scriptures that reverse this entire process for us. The Lord's way is the best, highest, and only way out. While God may certainly use someone else in your life to make you aware of specific issues and fears, the wonderful love of Christ still makes the most significant difference and sets you free from fear.

"You gain strength, courage, and confidence by every experience in which you really stop to look fear in the face. You are able to say to yourself, 'I lived through this horror. I can take the next thing that comes along.'"
—Eleanor Roosevelt

2

How Fear Works

Fear prepares us to react to danger. Once we sense a potential danger, our body releases hormones that either slow down or shut down different functions that are not needed for survival. Fear can also sharpen certain functions that might help us survive, such as eyesight. During a time of fear, our heart rate increases, and blood flows to muscles more quickly so we can run and act faster. Once the fear pathways are ramped up, the brain reacts in ways to help you survive. The brain reacts immediately to signals from the amygdala instead of more rational processing.

The Cleveland Clinic has been at the forefront of modern medicine since it was founded in 1921 and has introduced many medical firsts around the world, being ranked among the top hospitals in the United States. This is what the Cleveland Clinic writes about the function of the amygdala.

"The amygdala is a small, almond-shaped structure inside of your brain. When it comes to your survival, your amygdala is extremely important. This is the part of your brain that automatically detects danger. It also plays a role in behavior, emotional control, and learning. Fear is the main emotion that the amygdala is known to control. That's why your amygdala is so important to survival. It processes things you see or hear and uses that input to learn what's dangerous. If you encounter something similar in the future, your amygdala will cause you to feel fear or similar emotions. However, research shows that the amygdala contributes to more than just anxiety or fear. It also plays a role in aggression, learning through rewards and punishment, and handling and using memory. This allows you to remember how to do certain things without remembering how you learned them, like riding a bike or tying your shoes. It allows you to notice and store all the details. The brain stores all the details surrounding the danger — the sights, sounds, odors, time of day, weather, and so forth. These memories tend to be very durable, although they may also be fragmented."

These details can then later trigger the fear associated with it. The sights, sounds, and other details of a fearful event may bring back a memory, or they may cause us to feel afraid without consciously knowing why. Because these cues were associated with previous danger, the brain may see them as predicting a new threat.

In severe cases, this can result in post-traumatic stress disorder (PTSD). Virtually everyone has heard of that by now. For example, a soldier who experienced a bombing on a foggy day might find themselves panicking when the weather turns foggy — without even knowing why. Living under constant threat has serious health consequences, too. Fear weakens our immune system and can cause cardiovascular damage, gastrointestinal problems such as ulcers and irritable bowel syndrome, and decreased fertility. It can lead to accelerated aging and even premature death. I know this all sounds a bit scientific at this point, but again, we are talking about "how" fear works. This is important to understand.

Fear can impair the formation of long-term memories and cause damage to certain parts of the brain. This can make it even more difficult to regulate fear and can leave a person anxious most of the time. To someone in chronic fear, the world looks very scary, and their memories will certainly back up their fears. All of this can leave someone unable to act appropriately.

Fear is a human emotion that is triggered by a perceived threat. It is a basic survival mechanism that signals our bodies to respond to danger with an appropriate and helpful response. So, it is an essential part of keeping us safe. However, when people live in constant fear, whether from physical dangers in their environment or threats they perceive, they can also experience negative impacts in all these areas of their lives and even become incapacitated. That is where it really starts getting serious.

The origin of fear can be traced back to our adversary, the devil. As the father of lies and the accuser of the brethren, he seeks to instill fear, doubt, and confusion in our hearts and minds. Through his deceptive tactics, he aims to hinder our relationship with God, distort our understanding of God's love, and keep us trapped in a perpetual state of bondage. It can be a terrible situation if you let it.

Fear entered the world because of the sin that Adam and Eve got into in the Garden of Eden. When they disobeyed God's command and believed the lies of the serpent, fear entered their hearts, leading to shame, hiding, and separation from God. You can read all about this in the book of Genesis 3:8-10, "And they heard the sound of the LORD God walking in the garden in the cool of the day, and the man and his wife hid themselves from the presence of the LORD God among the trees of the garden. But the LORD God called to the man and said to him, "Where are you?" And he said, "I heard the sound of you in the garden, and I was afraid because I was naked, and I hid myself." Did you see what Adam said there? He said he was afraid.

This marked the beginning of the spiritual battle between good and evil, with fear as a weapon employed by the enemy. Make no doubt about it: the devil seeks to exert control over our lives by exploiting our vulnerabilities and planting seeds of fear in our minds. If he can just get you to believe his lies instead of God's truth, he can begin a lifetime of deception in your mind. Second Timothy 1:7 warns us, "For God gave us a spirit not of fear but of power and love and self-control." The spirit of fear does not come from God but is a tool the enemy uses to undermine our faith and hinder us from fulfilling God's purpose for our lives.

The Bible even says that satan, known as the accuser of the brethren, attempts to capitalize on our weaknesses and failures to provoke us with this fear and doubt. Revelation 12:10 describes him as the one "who accuses them day and night before our God." His goal is to keep us bound by guilt, shame, and the fear of punishment, preventing us from fully experiencing God's forgiveness and freedom. He has a constant mindset to prevent you from moving forward. His entire aim is to keep you bound so that you do not make any progress in the things of God. The devil simply does not play fair.

The devil continuously employs deception and lies to manipulate our thoughts and emotions, creating a continual atmosphere of fear. Jesus described satan as the father of lies in John 8:44, saying, "When he lies, he speaks out of his own character, for he is a liar and the father of lies." Did you catch that? Lying is part of the character of satan, and by distorting the truth of God's Word and sowing seeds of doubt, he seeks to undermine our trust in God and instill fear.

Of course, the ultimate aim of the devil is to steal from us, kill us, and utterly destroy us, according to John 10:10. Fear is one of his primary weapons to accomplish this. The enemy is desperate to keep us in a state of fear, attempting to hinder us, robbing us of peace, and constantly seeking to destroy our faith and relationship with God.

> *The devil continuously employs deception and lies to manipulate our thoughts and emotions, creating a continual atmosphere of fear.*

But just because fear originates from the enemy, we are not defenseless. Finally, here comes some good news! God has equipped us with spiritual weapons and armor to overcome the schemes of the devil. Ephesians 6:10-11 instructs us, "Finally, be strong in the Lord and in the strength of his might. Put on the whole armor of God, that you may be able to stand against the schemes of the devil."

The Truth is that by immersing ourselves in the Truth of God's Word, we can counter the lies of the enemy and find strength and comfort. Psalm 119:105 declares, "Your word is a lamp to my feet and a light to my path." And we certainly cannot forget prayer! Prayer is a powerful weapon against the enemy's tactics. Philippians 4:6-7 reminds us, "Do not be anxious about anything, but in everything by prayer and supplication with thanksgiving let your requests be made known to God. And the peace of God, which surpasses all understanding, will guard your hearts and your minds in Christ Jesus."

Through our ongoing personal relationship with Christ, we have authority over the enemy. James 4:7 encourages us, "Submit yourselves therefore to God. Resist the devil, and he will flee from you." So, we can plainly see that standing firm in our faith and resisting the lies and fears of the enemy will cause us to experience victory and freedom. Now, that is what God intended!

With fear, we find ourselves paralyzed and stuck, held captive by worries, anxieties, and insecurities. Fear whispers lies, convincing us of our inadequacy, bringing doubt, and stifling our progress. It erects barriers, limiting us, both external and internal. Fear keeps us trapped in the comfort of the familiar, deterring us from growth and robbing us of our futures.

It seems like this world is engulfed by fear, anxiety, and uncertainty, and it is crucial to understand these pitfalls and discover the abundant joy that comes with finding true peace. Fear, though a common human experience, has the potential to paralyze, hinder growth, and rob us of the fullness of life that God intends for us.

However, it is not a fate we are meant to accept. We were never designed to live that way! We do not have to live that way! And I declare right now that you are coming out, and you are coming through to victory over fear!

> *"Fear kills more dreams than*
> *failure ever will."*
> *—Suzy Kassem*

3

Nine Questions About Fear

It is important to ask questions. In their growing-up years, most of our children asked a lot of questions, but I remember a specific time when our oldest son, Joshua, was just old enough to really want to know how everything worked. He has always been a very inquisitive boy. Everywhere we went, he would constantly ask questions. When we would go to the zoo, he would ask, "Why do the giraffes have such long necks?" When we would walk through the mall, Joshua would ask, "Why are some of the lights white and some of the lights blue?" He even wanted to know how the clouds stayed up in the sky. There was a particular day when Joshua kept tugging on my wife's skirt, looking up at her with one question after another. On that day, Joshua seemed to have an unusually long barrage of questions. Eventually, my wife looked down at him and said, "Joshua, you sure do have a lot of questions today!" To which Joshua quickly responded, "Well, I have to ask a lot of questions because there are a lot of things that I do not know!" I think that about sums it up! Even as a young boy, my son knew that if he was going to gain information and learn this, he would need to ask a lot of questions. Joshua is now in his mid-30s, married, with four children of his own, and he still calls me from time to time to ask a few more questions. And I think we need to do the same thing.

Over quite a long period of time, I have had the opportunity to talk to many people about the fears that they face in life. There are certainly many different situations and things that people confront daily that are related to fear, but after thinking hard and long about many of those conversations through the years, I have done my very best to narrow down some of the main questions that I have heard from others. I have whittled the long list down to these nine questions. Let's take a closer look at these now to see if we can gain any additional information about how this whole thing works.

Question 1: What exactly is fear?

As I stated earlier, any decent dictionary would basically define fear as an unpleasant emotion caused by the belief that someone or something is dangerous. Something that is likely to cause pain or a threat. Fear is a feeling of anxiety concerning the outcome of something or the safety and well-being of someone or something. Fear is the understanding that there is a likelihood that something unwelcome is going to happen. No matter how you describe fear, there must be a clear understanding that fear must be kept in check in your life, or you will have damaging results. That is what this book is all about. I think it is also important to understand that there are two types of fear: healthy fear and unhealthy fear. We need to learn the difference between these two if we are going to have any success. At some point, almost everyone faces some kind of fear in their life. Some are more severe than others. The Bible is no stranger to the word "fear," and in fact, the Bible indicates to us many, many times to "fear not." If we count all the references to fear or variations of it in scripture, I believe that number skyrockets to well over 365 times. It is made very clear in scripture that God himself does not want people to walk in fear when they are faced with decisions and adversities. In the New Testament, the apostle Paul gave some great advice to a young man named Timothy. He said, "God has not given us the spirit of fear, but of power and of love and of a sound mind." 2 Timothy 1:7

Basically, what Paul was trying to say here is that God gives his followers a spirit of power, love, and a sound mind. Not fear.

Question 2: Why does fear come to us?

Fear is a natural human emotion that comes as a response to a perceived threat or danger. Fear can serve as a protective mechanism designed to keep us safe and alert in potentially harmful situations. Fear can manifest in various forms, such as fear of physical harm, fear of failure, fear of rejection, or fear of the unknown. Understanding why fear comes requires exploring its origins, purpose, and the intricacies of human experience.

Fear originates from a combination of factors. It is deeply rooted in us and stems from our survival instincts, which help us detect and respond to imminent dangers. Maybe you have known it as the "fight or flight" response, which triggers a cascade of physiological changes in our bodies, preparing us to either confront or escape threats.

Fear can arise from past experiences, traumatic events, or even conditioned responses. Negative experiences or witnessing others' struggles can shape our perception of the world and instill fear in us. Additionally, societal and cultural influences, upbringing, and learned behaviors can all contribute to the development of specific fears.

From a spiritual perspective, fear can also be influenced by the brokenness of the world. The Bible acknowledges the presence of fear and its destructive power, pointing to the reality of spiritual forces that seek to steal, kill, and destroy us (John 10:10). The enemy, satan, often exploits fear to hinder our faith, distort our perceptions, and prevent us from living in the fullness of God's plan for our lives.

Question 3: What is the purpose of fear?

As I just mentioned, there is a healthy fear that comes with benefits and an unhealthy fear that only brings trouble. Healthy fear can literally save your life. Just knowing the physical damage that could come from an automobile accident may cause you to put your seatbelt on, which is a good thing. If you know the dangers of a vehicle being hit by a train, it will probably keep you off the train tracks. If you have a fresh understanding of your mind that a hot stove will burn your hand, you are a lot less likely to touch the hot stove. Having the desire to remain safe from harm may cause you to take action that saves your life. Looking at the track record of other people and other situations, you can understand that it would be easy to develop a proper fear of snakes. If you have a proper understanding of this kind of fear, you will most likely not go out and pick up a poisonous snake, which, again, is a good thing. God has built into each of us the ability to discern when something could be harmful to us.

We should pay close attention to that part. A healthy fear can heighten and sharpen your senses and become very beneficial. You may have heard of this referred to as a "fight or flight" sense.

Fear serves a vital purpose in our lives when it is taken and understood properly. Its primary function is to alert us to potential threats, enabling us to respond appropriately for self-preservation. In dangerous situations, fear triggers the release of adrenaline, preparing us for action. It prompts us to evaluate risks, make informed decisions, and take necessary precautions. After all, once you have put your hand on a hot stove, you find out very quickly that you don't ever want to do that again. So, there is a specific purpose for fear in that it keeps us from repeating stupid mistakes and injuring ourselves. But fear can also be taken too far. In some cases, way too far!

Fear acts as a warning system, helping us recognize and address underlying issues. It can signal areas of our lives that require attention, healing, or growth. For example, the fear of failure might indicate a need to develop self-confidence or overcome perfectionism.

Healthy fear is a lot like a red light on your car's dashboard. It may be warning you or cautioning you that have some danger ahead or something that is about to happen. Healthy fear is the kind of fear that sometimes will slow you down to give you a little more time to assess the situation before doing something reckless, stupid, or dangerous.

On the other hand, unhealthy fear is a fear without any basis. There is no real threat of physical, financial, or spiritual danger, yet you feel completely frozen and fearful. This can include thoughts or feelings that something bad may happen but is completely based on the unknown. Based on complete speculation. Most of the time, unhealthy fear is negative and tends to hold you back. It keeps you from advancing and doing the things that God desires you to do. Healthy fear gives you a sense of respect for God and what is just ahead on the road. Unhealthy fear has a lack of respect for God and does not consider His goodness in the equation. A healthy fear is one that is from God and benefits you. Unhealthy fear will cause you to stop advancing, growing, and developing. Unhealthy fear will continuously cause you to doubt everything around you and keep you from growing spiritually mature in Christ. Listen to what the Bible says here, and Isaiah 41:13, "For I, the LORD your God, hold your right hand; it is I who say to you, "Fear not, I am the one who helps you." When we surrender our fears to God, we invite Him to work in and through us, trusting in His provision, protection, and guidance.

Question 4: How long does fear last?

The duration of fear varies from person to person and depends on various factors, such as the intensity of the fear, the individual's resilience, and the steps taken to address and overcome it. Fear can lie dormant and then be triggered by specific circumstances or events and retreat once the perceived threat has passed. However, fear can also become chronic and persistent, deeply ingrained in your thought patterns and behaviors. That is where the danger of fear really begins.

The duration of fear is influenced by our responses to it. If we continually avoid or suppress our fears, they may persist and even intensify over time. However, actively confronting and addressing our fears can lead to their resolution and eventual freedom. It is essential to recognize that overcoming fear is a process that requires intentional effort, self-reflection, and reliance on God's strength.

Question 5: Is there any escape from fear?

Yes, there is hope for escaping the grip of fear. If there were no escape from fear, then there would be no purpose in reading this book. The good news is you absolutely can escape fear! While fear may be a natural human emotion, it does not have to control or define our lives. God has provided a way for us to overcome fear and experience true freedom.

The escape from fear begins with acknowledging its presence and its impact on our lives. It requires a willingness to confront our fears head-on rather than avoiding or suppressing them. We must recognize that fear often distorts our perception and limits our potential. By taking intentional steps toward overcoming fear, we can move toward a life marked by courage, faith, and victory.

Remember how we were talking about good fear and bad fear? Well, it seems like this is an appropriate time to make sure that you also understand that having a healthy fear of the Lord is biblical and beneficial. It leads to wisdom! This is one kind of fear that you don't want to escape! Listen to what the Bible says in Psalm 111:10 "The fear of the LORD is the beginning of wisdom; all those who practice it have a good understanding. His praise endures forever!" And check out this verse from Proverbs

14:27, "The fear of the LORD is a fountain of life, that one may turn away from the snares of death."

So, even though it is proper to want to escape the bad kind of fear, it is always good to hold the Lord in a place of reverence and awe in your heart. Understanding the proper balance between these two will help keep you from drifting away spiritually. After all, God is the creator and giver of life, and he holds the entire universe together. So, it is important to maintain a godly fear and reverence and understand that this is healthy. It is a good thing to maintain a heart of reverence, honor, and praise for God. After all, he is a mighty God and worthy of our praise.

Question 6: How do I get away from fear?

Escaping from fear involves a multi-faceted approach that addresses the physical, emotional, psychological, and spiritual dimensions of fear. I will go into this in much greater detail throughout the book, but for now, here are some key strategies to help you get away from fear:

- Identify and acknowledge your fears: Take time to reflect on the specific fears that hold you back. Be honest with yourself and face them without judgment or condemnation.

- Seek God's perspective: Turn to God's Word to gain His perspective on fear. The Bible provides numerous verses that encourage us to trust in God's faithfulness, seek His wisdom, and find refuge in Him. Meditate on these scriptures and allow God's truth to replace fear-driven thoughts. We will go into this in much greater detail throughout this book.

- Prayer and surrender: Engage in regular prayer, casting your fears, worries, and anxieties before God. Surrender your fears to Him, trusting that He is a good God and has a perfect plan for your life.

- Renew your mind: Cultivate a mindset focused on truth, positivity, and faith. Replace negative thoughts with affirmations rooted in God's promises. Surround yourself with uplifting and encouraging influences, such as reading inspiring books, listening to sermons, and connecting with supportive Christian friends and leaders.

- Take action: Confront your fears step by step. Break them down into manageable goals and take small, intentional actions to face them. Gradually exposing yourself to what you fear can help desensitize the emotional response and build confidence.

- Seek support: It can be important to reach out to trusted friends, family members, or mentors who can provide support and encouragement on your journey. Share your struggles, seek guidance, and learn from others who have overcome similar fears. Personally, this was a big step for me. I had tried on my own for many years to overcome some of these things, but it was not until I reached out to some people around me that I ultimately started getting a handle on things.

- Professional help: If your fears significantly impact your daily life or mental well-being, consider seeking professional help. Therapists, counselors, or support groups can provide valuable tools and guidance for overcoming deep-rooted fears. If you take this route, I strongly encourage you to go to a godly therapist or counselor. Someone who actively uses the Word of God as a firm basis for their advice and help.

Question 7: Can I prevent fear from coming again?

While it may be impossible to prevent fear from ever resurfacing again, you can develop strategies to manage and mitigate its impact. By actively practicing self-awareness, self-care, and reliance on God, you can become more resilient and equip yourself to face future fears. Here are some practices that can help:

- Continual self-reflection: Regularly assess your thoughts, emotions, and triggers that contribute to fear. Stay vigilant and address any new fears promptly. This is so important.

- Strengthen your faith: Invest in your relationship with God through prayer, Bible study, and worship. Deepen your understanding of His character and promises, finding solace in His presence and guidance.

- Practice self-care: Prioritize self-care activities that nourish your mind, body, and spirit. Engage in activities that bring joy, relaxation, and restoration. Something as simple as adequate rest can contribute greatly to your emotional well-being and ability to overcome fear. My wife often says that if you just take three deep breaths and drink a tall glass of water, most of the issues you face can be resolved quickly. It is a matter of preparing yourself and coming to the realization that it is going to be okay in the end.

- Surround yourself with a supportive community: Develop relationships with individuals who encourage and uplift you. It is always going to be difficult to move in a forward or upward direction if you only hang out with people who are pulling you down. Share your journey with trusted friends or mentors who can provide accountability, wisdom, and support. I have a close friend who has meant the world to me for this very reason. I know beyond a shadow of a doubt that I can go to him and share anything that I am facing, and he will encourage me and help me. It is extremely comforting to know that you have someone that you can go to.

- Stay committed to personal growth: Engage in ongoing personal development and growth. Continuously challenge yourself to step outside your comfort zone, embracing new experiences and perspectives.

Question 8: Can I be completely free of fear?

While complete freedom from fear may be a lifelong journey, it is possible to experience significant liberation from its grip. I remember a time when my wife and I took a trip to go snow skiing in Colorado. We had already skied for a couple of days and then decided to go into town to look at some of the cute little shops there. I remember a store that we went into that was full of different kinds of decorative signs to hang in your house. One of those signs read, "Cleaning up after your children while they are still playing is like trying to shovel snow while it is still snowing!" So, I think it is important to understand that just because you are embarking on the journey to tackle fear once and for all in your life, you will still have an adversary who wants to pile more fear on top of you as you go. Our enemy, the devil, has a lifelong dream and goal of continuously attempting to steal from you, kill you, and destroy you. Fortunately, we are also firmly placed in God's hands, and we have the wonderful Word of God to combat and overcome these fears. As we grow in our faith, deepen our understanding of God's love, and apply practical strategies to overcome fear, we can experience substantial breakthroughs.

It is essential to note that freedom from fear does not necessarily mean the absence of fear altogether. Instead, it involves developing a healthy relationship with God so that fear no longer controls or paralyzes us. We can learn to acknowledge fear's presence, discern when it is necessary and when it is irrational, and respond accordingly in the face of it. I do not remember who said this, but I remember seeing a great quote that said, "Peace is not the absence of fear, but rather the presence of God, in the midst of your fear!" Do you need to fully understand that God is with you, God is for you, and he is not going to leave you alone. He said that he would never leave you or forsake you. That is great news!

Question 9: How do I obtain freedom from fear?

Again, 2 Timothy 1:7 states, "For God gave us a spirit not of fear but of power and love and self-control." This verse highlights that, as believers, we are given a spirit of power, love, and self-control by God. It implies that through the empowerment of the Holy Spirit, we can overcome fear in our lives. Psalm 34:4 goes on to say, "I sought the LORD, and he answered me and delivered me from all my fears." This verse expresses the psalmist's experience of seeking the Lord and being delivered from all fears. Although it does not mention a specific timeline, it assures us that seeking God's help can lead to the removal of fear from our lives.

And finally, Isaiah 41:10 says, "Fear not, for I am with you; be not dismayed, for I am your God; I will strengthen you, I will help you, I will uphold you with my righteous right hand." This verse reassures us of God's presence and support in the face of fear. It emphasizes that God will strengthen and uphold us, implying that His presence enables us to overcome fear over time. So, while these verses do not explicitly mention a timeframe, they provide comfort, encouragement, and the assurance of God's help in conquering fear. Overcoming fear is a journey that involves trust, faith, and a consistent reliance on God's strength and guidance.

While the Bible does not necessarily contain an explicit verse that states it takes a while to get rid of fear from one's life, there are certain verses like these that provide guidance and encouragement in overcoming fear.

Here are some additional principles that may answer the question further:

- Seek God's truth: Ground yourself in God's Word, seeking His truth to counteract the lies and distortions that fear presents. Meditate on scriptures that highlight His faithfulness, love, and power.

- Cultivate faith: Develop an unwavering trust in God's goodness. Anchor your faith in His promises, believing that He is with you, for you, and will never forsake you.

- Be vulnerable with God: Allow yourself to be vulnerable before God. Surrender your fears, insecurities, and weaknesses to Him, inviting His strength to work through your vulnerabilities.

- Practice gratitude: Cultivate a grateful heart, focusing on the blessings and provisions in your life. Gratitude helps shift our perspective from fear to trust and fosters a positive outlook.

- Embrace self-compassion: Extend grace and compassion to yourself. Recognize that fear is a common human experience, and it is okay to feel afraid. Treat yourself with kindness and gentleness as you navigate through fear.

- Continue to develop a prayer life: Regularly engage in prayer, pouring out your fears and concerns to God. Seek His guidance, wisdom, and peace as you navigate through challenging circumstances.

- Renew your mind: Replace fear-driven thoughts with truth-filled affirmations. Meditate on positive and empowering scriptures that counteract fear and build confidence in God's strength.

- Step out in faith: Take intentional steps to face your fears, even if they are small at first. As you step out in faith, trust that God is with you, empowering you to overcome and grow.

- Surround yourself with support: Stick with like-minded people who encourage and uplift you. Seek guidance and support from mentors, friends, or support groups who can walk alongside you on your journey to freedom.

- Embrace a lifestyle of growth: Commit to lifelong growth and personal development. Engage in practices that nurture your spiritual, emotional, and mental well-being. Pursue learning, self-reflection, and the pursuit of your God-given purpose.

Ok, enough of that! So far, we have been discussing the differences between healthy fear and unhealthy fear, but from this point on, we are primarily going to deal with the ugly stuff. That is the reason I am really writing this book. So, moving forward, we are going to go a lot deeper into the evils of fear and the methods to be free from it. I will give you a little warning in advance that some of the material might make you a bit mad, mainly because you will begin to recognize how fear operates in your life on a regular basis and to what degree fear already has a grip on you. It can be a little upsetting when you realize how free you could have been all along. But the good news is that when you start seeing the particulars of fear at work in your life, you will be in a great position to finally free yourself once and for all! Here we go!

"Fear is the glue that keeps you stuck.
Faith is the solvent that sets you free." — Shannon L. Alder

4

The Curse of Overthinking

I want to talk about overthinking for a few minutes. This is so important! This is one of the primary things that I had overcome in my life. Overthinking is one of the easiest and worst ways to allow fear to enter our lives. **When you are overthinking, you are literally thinking about the problem over and over instead of concentrating on the goodness of God.** You are only thinking about the problem. You are digging the hole deeper and deeper, not understanding that you have to stop digging to ever escape. It is a cycle of thinking that only leads to hurt and problems. **Instead of trusting in the promises of God, we see the problem as bigger than the promise.** Overthinking is usually scenario-based, meaning that it is easy for you to think of all scenarios and situations in which something will not work. An overthinker sees the end result as an utter failure before the first step is taken. It is pre-determining an outcome of doom and despair before even knowing what success looks like. Ouch!

Overthinking is like having a debate with yourself about things that haven't even materialized yet. Seriously, the debate is only with yourself, and it is only in your head, in your mind.

It is a lot like being in court. Except in this court, you are the judge and get to determine the final decision about which way things will go, but you are also the prosecutor and the defense attorney. You are arguing all sides of the case with yourself, even though all the evidence is still unfounded. At this point, there is not enough information to make a solid decision, but you still feel the need to argue both sides of the case — with yourself! In the end, it is a complete waste of time, but only your time at the moment. Later, we will see that it also begins to waste other people's time as well. Maybe you have been in a situation where you are driving alone in your own car, constantly rehearsing all sides of the argument over and over. Have you ever done that? Have you ever gotten to the point where you are basically debating yourself over a certain thing as you are driving down the road by yourself? Have you ever caught yourself beginning to say things out loud? If you have, this is the chapter for you! By the way, I have done that many times! You are in good company!

Keep in mind that there is a vast difference between thinking and overthinking. It is like the difference between cooking something or overcooking something. Baking something or over-baking something. Who would not want a wonderfully baked fresh cherry pie? Yet, probably no one wants a freshly burnt cherry pie! You see, the difference between baking and burning is simply a matter of how much time is spent. Baking for a certain amount of time can be great, resulting in some delicious food everyone wants to eat. But if you continue to bake the same food for a much longer period of time, you end up with burnt food. It is really just a matter of doing it or overdoing it! Thinking is great and helps us become aware of the critical components that affect our lives. Thinking helps us formulate ideas for the decisions that we need to make every day. One of the differences between thinking and overthinking is that thinking ultimately makes a decision and moves forward, while overthinking never reaches a conclusion. It is simply endless. Each question in your mind only opens the door to four more questions, and the cycle just repeats until something breaks. The problem is you are the one who breaks!

That is the way that overthinking allows fear into your life. I know; I come from a great long line of overthinkers! Operating this way focuses your entire attention on what is wrong instead of on what is right. It forces you to look at the negative rather than the positive. Overthinking also occupies much of your time by rehashing negative scenarios rather than reading God's Word or talking to Him about it. It completely excludes God from the equation. It is like putting God on the back burner. So, even though God Himself is sitting there waiting with the answers and is ready to provide them, you cannot even see that if you are overthinking.

Overthinking, in its various forms, can grip your heart and mind, preventing you from stepping into your purpose and living a life of fulfillment. This kind of fear paralyzes you. It stops you in your tracks. It literally steals your joy and hope. It keeps you trapped in a cycle of anxiety and worry. But scripture tells us in Proverbs 12:25, "Anxiety in a man's heart weighs him down, but a good word makes him glad."

We went on vacation to Mexico one time, and on that trip, I got to go scuba diving. I had grown up in Florida many years ago and had been certified as a scuba diver while I lived there, but now it had been many years since I had been on a dive.

Fortunately, I was able to take a diving refresher course and then get back into the water again. The kind of dive that I was on that day was to go see the large sea turtles underwater. I had never experienced anything quite like that, and honestly, I was quite excited to get started. One of the things I did not realize about this kind of dive is that it takes place inside an underwater current. After you jump out of the boat with all your scuba gear on, you then have to swim down to about 80 feet underwater, where the underwater current is. It is a very strong current, almost like an underwater river. I was surprised that it took so much effort to swim into it. As soon as I swam from the regular ocean water into the current stream, I was immediately whisked away at a much greater speed. This was all part of the trip because this is how sea turtles travel such great distances. It was a great dive that day, and I had lots of fun; then came the part when I had to swim back out of the current to get to the boat again. This proved to be a lot harder than I thought. It was not just a normal casual swim; it required some real effort to get out of that current. A lot more than I expected. So, when I say that fear has a way of keeping you trapped in a cycle of anxiety and worry, this is kind of how I picture it. It is not enough to just casually swim away from overthinking, anxiety, and worry. It takes a little effort on your part to break free from this cycle. From the current that you may be stuck in.

Ultimately, overthinking leads us into the grips of fear, where it becomes much harder to ever decide or move forward with anything. **It is what is commonly referred to as "paralysis by analysis."** It paralyzes you and stops you in your tracks so that you can take a lot of time to analyze every possible detail of every possible situation in every possible scenario at every possible time with every possible person. If you were a mathematician, you could think of this as trying to solve an impossible equation. Have you ever seen one of those movies where there is a math teacher with a giant chalkboard that is full of numbers, symbols, and equations? If you are not a math genius, you'll just see the chalkboard as showing something impossible. That is what overthinking is like. It is like walking up to that giant chalkboard full of equations that is 20 feet tall and 40 feet wide and attempting to solve that problem, except you are not a mathematician.

Overthinking has a way of distorting our perceptions and deceiving us into believing false narratives.

We need to be honest here; we need thinkers in this world. The thinkers are the ones who design things and make sure that things are safe. Would you rather cross the river on the newly constructed bridge that was designed and built by thinkers or designed and built by those happy-go-lucky people I mentioned earlier? Because the happy-go-lucky people in charge of designing the bridge might just say, "Let's just try this, I'm sure it will work out fine! What could possibly go wrong?" However, the thinking person will design the bridge with many questions in mind. They will take everything into consideration. They will think about the type of bolts to use to connect the steel beams. They will think about the thickness and load-bearing capacity of those steel beams. They will think about the tensile strength of the concrete that is used to hold the beams in place on the shoreline. They will think about the tension on the wire that supports the main frame. They will think about the thickness of the concrete or asphalt that is used to pave the road on top of the bridge. They will consider all the weight-bearing factors to ensure that every single element of the bridge works properly and will stay in place for decades to come. So, which person would you prefer to design and build the bridge? What about airline pilots? Consider them for just a second. Would you knowingly and willingly get on a jet airplane to go somewhere if you knew the pilot was a happy-go-lucky pilot? Someone who had the mindset of "I'm sure I can fly this thing; how hard can it be?" Or would you prefer to have someone who is extremely knowledgeable about every single button and knob in the cockpit? Someone who walked around the exterior of the plane before takeoff to ensure that every part of the aircraft was working properly. Someone who went through a flight safety checklist to ensure that every single element of the flight had been considered. Which pilot would you rather have? I think we all know the answers to these questions, and it certainly sheds light on the fact that there is a definite place for thinkers in this world. We need thinkers! But again, there is a big difference between thinking and overthinking. Overthinking leads to fear, and fear bogs you down and keeps you indecisive. There needs to be a balance. I want the pilot to thoroughly check out the plane, but if it got to the point where he had been checking it out for nine or ten hours, I may feel differently. That length of time would then cause me to completely miss my destination, and that would be pointless.

Overthinking has a way of distorting our perceptions and deceiving us into believing false narratives. Then, fear can manipulate our thoughts, influence our decisions, and hinder us altogether. But, the Bible says, "For God gave us a spirit not of fear but of power and love and self-control" (2 Timothy 1:7, ESV). We can plainly see that God did not give us fear. In fact, fear and faith are in constant opposition to each other. Fear is constantly trying to erode our faith, causing doubt and unbelief to overshadow the promises of God. We must discover the importance of understanding faith and trusting God's unfailing love. Look at what the Psalmist said in Psalm 56:3, "But when I am afraid, I put my trust in you." When should you put your trust in God? Whenever you are afraid! Whenever fear strikes! But we also must understand that this is a choice we each have. The opportunity to be afraid can be presented to you, but you do not have to participate. Just because something comes to you does not mean you have to receive it. Just because it is offered does not mean that it must be accepted. I remember a time when my wife and I had just returned home from shopping at the grocery store and parked the car in the driveway. Just by habit, we both walked to the mailbox to check for mail. Once I opened the mailbox, I saw that there were quite a few pieces of mail for us. I did what any good guy would do and began flipping through the mail to see what was important and what was just junk mail. One of the pieces of mail was from an address that I did not recognize, so I quickly opened the envelope to see what it was. To my surprise, it was full of pornography. It was not even hidden but plainly visible upon opening the envelope. I quickly shut the envelope and handed it to my wife. Once I told her what was inside the envelope, we quickly went inside the house and shredded the entire envelope immediately. We did not ask to receive that envelope. We did not order the envelope. We had no idea that the envelope had come to us. The envelope was presented to us, but we did not have to participate in it or receive it. We were able to quickly shred it and completely do away with the threat and harm that could have come from that information. Again, it was presented to us, but we did not have to receive it.

A lot of the time, fear will be based on our senses. Our senses provide us with evidence of things that we can see, hear, smell, touch, and taste. The only problem is that fear tends to exploit these senses and blow them out of proportion. Fear exaggerates. Fear can also be self-contained, already arriving with all the evidence needed to accept it. Evidence that is based on past failures. Evidence that is based on other people who have problems in life. Even people who have died with the same thing the doctors have told you that you have. Business ventures that failed for someone else while you are currently following that same business plan. Friends that are your age who have just experienced financial failure in life. And the list goes on and on. Fear is always quick to show you what went wrong with other people, situations, and even your own past to set up a failure for your future. **Fear operates in the present but utilizes the past and prepares to destroy your future.** But, you have to let it. So, how in the world do you ever get ahead of this thing and make the right choices?

For me to answer that question, I absolutely must talk to you right now about your "Let Switch!" That's right, your "Let Switch!" You have a "Let Switch" on the inside of you. Not a light switch, but a Let Switch. You already know what a light switch is, right? It is a switch that turns on or off a light. And you already know that if you turn a light switch on, the power is then released through the switch, travels to the lightbulb, and causes the light to come on. As soon as the switch is switched, power is released, resulting in light. Well, if a light switch turns a light on or off, then it stands to reason that a Let Switch would certainly turn on or off a LET. Your Let! Allow me to explain. A Let is a Choice! You have a choice to Let or to Let Not! Those are Bible terms. Let me give you a couple of examples…

In the book of Philippians, the Lord said to "Let" this mind be in you, which was also in Jesus…" You have to choose to Let it! The Bible also says in John 14:1 that you should "Let Not" your heart be troubled…" Again, your choice. You will see this all through the Bible as you are reading. In fact, every single time you hear the Word of God, you are faced with a choice to *Let* or *Let Not* that message work in your life.

Here is another one… How about what is said in Matthew 5:16? "Let your light so shine before men, that they may see your good works, and glorify your Father which is in heaven."

For your light to shine, you have to turn your light switch on, and you do that by turning your Let Switch on! It is scripturally correct to let your light shine. It is scriptural to Let Not your heart be troubled, and it is scriptural to Let this mind be in you.

The problem is that even though it is a switch that you can choose to turn on or off, some people still treat it like it is a dimmer! "Oh, I am just going to partially choose to obey God," "I will follow God's plan just a little bit," and "I will read the Word of God just once in a while." That is why you get so frustrated so quickly. Inside yourself, you want to shine a bright light, but it is still a little dim. At some point in your life, you must understand that turning a switch on is a commitment. A dimmer is not a commitment! The whole idea behind a dimmer is that it is variable. It depends. It depends on how much light you want. You could choose a little bit of light, or you could use a lot of light, or you could simply choose anything in between. There is no commitment to using a dimmer. How you use a dimmer depends on your current situation. No pun intended! It is variable. A switch is a commitment to either be on or off. You get to choose what you will do with what you hear. You have an opportunity to overcome fear in your life, but you need to *choose* to do it. You flip your own switch.

**Fear seems to always present choices,
but they are never good ones.**

Fear seems to always present choices, but they are never good ones. Fear always makes sure that the risky side of things is always present, even when there is a golden opportunity. It sounds something like this: "There is a wonderful new job opportunity waiting for you that will nearly double your salary, but it may not work out at all, and then you might get stuck between jobs without any income if things go wrong. Then what will you do to feed your family?" It also sounds like this: "If you were to take Friday off of work, you would have this wonderful, nice long weekend to spend with your family, but your boss might also be upset that you took advantage of the situation and decide to let you go on Monday when you get back." "If you invest some money now, while this stock is very low, you could make a lot of money, but this stock may continue to go down, and you could also lose it all." "If you reach out to those new people in the neighborhood, you could make some wonderful new friends, but they may not really like you, and then it would be awkward every time you see them in the future." "I heard that there is a big sale down at the local department store, and this would be a great time to get some new clothes, but they might already be sold out of your size, and then it would just be a wasted trip costing you much-needed gas money." Did you notice anything about all those statements? Did you notice that with each positive thing presented, there was also a "but?" See, fear always makes sure to present the negative along with the positive. With fear, it is never just good news; it is always good news and bad news, with the emphasis always being on the bad! Fear uses the bad news to attempt to outweigh the good news and once again keep you from taking any action at all. **Fear just wants you to remain stagnant**. To stand still and not make any progress.

Now, what I did not tell you was that those hypothetical situations that I just listed were not hypothetical at all. Each of those situations was personally presented to me over a period of time. In each situation, I was so bound by fear that I always chose the bad news part of the equation. I did not make the job change because I was scared that something would go wrong, and I would not be able to feed my family. I did not take that Friday off to have a long weekend with my family because I was scared that my boss would let me go. I did not make the investment in that stock because I was scared that I would lose at all. I did not reach out to those new people in our neighborhood because I feared rejection. I did not take advantage of the big sale at the department store because I was scared that they would be out of my size. I'm not kidding! And if you are the kind of person who has also walked in fear throughout your life, you will easily be able to relate to those situations. They are very real situations for someone who is an overthinker. I was that overthinker. I know this is embarrassing for me, but it is also worth it if I can help you overcome these same kinds of things. These horrible, debilitating thoughts. Of course, if you are of the happy-go-lucky variety and you are still reading this book for sheer entertainment purposes, you have probably just confirmed that the rest of us are crazy! There is probably a little truth mixed in there, but our craziness has only come about because we have walked in so much fear.

So, what I am saying is that fear always makes sure that bad news is included somewhere along the way. Fear has a "but," and if you accept that "but," then it becomes your "but!" And then your "but" is always in the way! Sometimes, you just have to get your "but" out of the way! I know it sounds funny, but it is true.

Now that we have talked about a few phrases and how fear always gets its "but" in the way let's go a little further. Fear has a continual voice, too. It does not want to let up or give you a break. Fear always tries to take you much further down the road than you ever intended to go. Listen to some of the other ways that fear can talk to you and see if you can identify and relate to any of these kinds of things. I will give you a little warning that these next phrases might make you mad! Especially when you realize how common they are and how often you hear these things in your mind. You need to hear this because this is how fear talks to you. Fear does not play fair!

Fear says things like this: What will you do now? You can't make it from here. After you lose this job, how will you feed your family? Your parents didn't do well financially, and neither will you. You have already passed your peak; you never could make it happen. You will struggle all your life with money. Your expenses will always exceed your income. Just go ahead and prepare for lack. The more you follow God, the worse it gets. You can't have nice things; you are just destined to live, scraping the bottom of the barrel. Others will succeed, but you will not. Your time is now past; you've already missed the opportunities for your success. You'll never get out of debt. You'll never have a nice car. Expenses will continue to rise, your income will continue to decrease, and it won't get any better. Better clothes for your kids and family — forget about it. Your business is going to flop, so why even try? Can't you see by now that you don't have what it takes to start a business? Even if you got some money, you would lose it quickly. From this point on, it will just be one problem after another, one breakdown after another, one failure after another. Don't you get it? You are too old, inexperienced, under-educated, too financially burdened, too risky for promotion, and too medically challenged, and nobody wants you. You are too old, too young, too overweight, too thin, too tall, too short. Don't you think it's time you face reality; You're just not going to make it. If it's not working by now, God doesn't want you to prosper. Let's face it, you are destined to struggle, and so are your children after you."

I am sorry to have to list things like that, but it is important for you to hear what fear sounds like so you can easily see it coming *and do something about it*. I do not even like typing those words. In fact, I am literally crying right now while I am typing because those things are so very real to someone who struggles with fear. I have done this for so many years, and it always seems a little hard to explain. Fear tries to make your future appear doubtful and to seem unpredictable, unsettled, unstable, unsteady, and uncertain.

If your mind is constantly thinking about failure, it will ultimately paralyze you and keep you from pursuing your dreams and stepping out in faith. And one of the worst parts about all this is that those around you will not necessarily understand your plight. It would be like someone who is bound to a wheelchair, without the ability to walk, but being surrounded by people who can walk. It would be like those walking people constantly saying to the wheelchair-bound person, "Just get up and walk, it's easy," "What's the problem, just get up and walk and leave the wheelchair behind." To someone who is not bound by these fears, it can look and seem so simple and so easy. But to the person who is still in fear, it feels impossible. I know this feeling all too well. But there is a way out!

We need to confront the crippling nature of this fear and learn how to embrace failure as a steppingstone to growth and success. Instead of looking at failure as the end of the road, we need to turn it around and begin thinking of failure as the elimination of another option that did not work. It does not mean it is the end; it just means we are starting again from here. The Scriptures encourage us in Joshua 1:9, "Have I not commanded you? Be strong and courageous. Do not be frightened, and do not be dismayed, for the Lord your God is with you wherever you go." You see, there is a way out, but the way out is not just to give up. We must determine inside ourselves to keep going. We must learn to rely on the Holy Spirit at work on the inside of us, strengthening us, leading us, guiding us, and showing us the way out. No one wants to let fear strain and break their relationships with others, but we must purposely *choose* not to let it. If we are going to maintain our ability to connect with others authentically, then it will be up to us to discover the transforming power of love and forgiveness and learn to shed fear altogether.

The Scriptures remind us in 1 John 4:18, "There is no fear in love, but perfect love casts out fear. For fear has to do with punishment, and whoever fears has not been perfected in love." I tell you, that is one powerful verse of scripture! Do you see what it said? It is said that perfect love has removed fear. So, let me ask you this question: who or what is perfect love? I think you know the answer to that already. Jesus Christ is perfect love! So, that verse is telling us that where there is perfect love, fear cannot exist. **There is no fear in love.** If we want to have less fear in our lives or no fear in our lives, we need to get to know Jesus a lot better than we do right now.

Second Peter 1:2 puts it this way; "May grace and peace be multiplied to you in the knowledge of God and of Jesus our Lord." You can now clearly see that grace and peace can be multiplied to you and in you through the knowledge of God and of Jesus. The better you get to know Jesus; the more grace and peace you will experience in your life and the less fear and anxiety you will experience in your life.

That is why one of the biggest things that fear tries to do in our lives is rob us of God's peace! The Scriptures assure us in Philippians 4:6-7, "Do not be anxious about anything, but in everything by prayer and supplication with thanksgiving let your requests be made known to God. And the peace of God, which surpasses all understanding, will guard your hearts and your minds in Christ Jesus." That is so comforting to hear. It is wonderful to know that the peace of God will guard your heart and your mind. That is really good news! I mean, who would not want more peace? We all do. When you put some of these scriptures together and read them in context, it becomes crystal clear that the more you submit your life to God and resist the devil, the better you get to know Jesus, the more fear will leave your life and be replaced with the peace of God. Now, that is something you can grab a hold of. True freedom from fear is found in surrendering our fears and anxieties to God. By accepting God's goodness and embracing His plans for our lives. Scripture encourages us in 1 Peter 5:6-7, "Humble yourselves, therefore, under the mighty hand of God so that at the proper time he may exalt you, casting all your anxieties on him, because he cares for you."

---

*Overcoming fear is a
journey of faith.*

Overcoming fear is a journey of faith. By walking in faith, we will begin to discover the power that comes by stepping out in faith, relying on God's guidance, and embracing the unknown with confidence. The Bible says in Proverbs 3:5-6, "Trust in the LORD with all your heart and do not lean on your own understanding. In all your ways, acknowledge him, and he will make straight your paths."

Living a life free from fear will bring a fearless mindset rooted in the truth of God's Word. Again, 2 Timothy 1:7 says, "For God gave us a spirit not of fear but of power and love and self-control." I know I keep using that Bible verse, but it is so important for you to understand that verse.

The ultimate goal is to *abide* in the peace of God, walking in His presence every day and resting in His love. To delve into the practices of prayer, meditation, and intimacy with God, which all lead us to a place of deep peace and security. Scripture encourages us in Isaiah 26:3, "You keep him in perfect peace whose mind is stayed on you because he trusts in you." I've always loved that scripture. I think it is just very comforting to know that God will keep me in perfect peace if I just keep my mind fixed on Him. I think that is so awesome! Once you start putting some of these things together, you begin to see that you can completely trust God. You can completely trust His ways and his methods. You will begin to see that He only intends good things for you and will never hurt or harm you in any way. Fear tries to be a force to hinder our growth. It tries to steal our peace and limit our potential. But through the power of God's Word and a deeper trust in His faithfulness, we can overcome fear and live a life filled with joy, peace, and purpose.

One of the key factors in eliminating fear from your life is **simply learning to trust God more**. I know it seems like I keep saying some of the same things over and over, but I believe it is very important to get this ingrained deep inside of us. Again, we all need this. We need to learn that it is okay to hear something more than once. If you think about it, you know that you would have absolutely no problem listening to the same song several times a day or putting it on continuous repeat because you really like that song. Imagine what would happen if we did the same thing with scriptures from the Bible. Imagine if spending time with God, reading God's Word, and talking to Him became so important to you that you would do anything not to miss it. Imagine what it would be like if we treated our Bible the way we treat our mobile phones. What if we left home for work but then remembered we left our Bible on the kitchen counter? What if we then turned back to get it because it was too important to be without it for even part of the day? Ouch! I know that might be a little hard-hitting, but maybe we need to hear it. If you spend more time staring at your mobile phone screen than you do staring at the Word of God, you might want to reevaluate some of your life priorities. **If you can spend hours every day swiping through endless social media screens on your phone and never flipping through the pages of the Bible, you might want to rethink some things.** How in the world would you ever expect to renew your mind to the things of God and give yourself the power to overcome fear if you are not even willing to take a closer look at what the Bible says?

I read something one day that totally changed my perspective. My father-in-law used to be a Gideon. The Gideons are a group of Christian believers dedicated to making the Word of God available to everyone. If you've ever been in a hotel room, almost anywhere in the world, and opened the drawer on your nightstand, you have inevitably seen a Bible that has been placed there by the Gideons. If you open that Bible, on the first few pages, you will see a description that the Gideons have given the Word of God. It is powerful in its description of the Bible. Here is the text that appears at the beginning of a Gideon Bible:

> *"The Bible contains the mind of God, the state of man, the way of salvation, the doom of sinners, and the happiness of believers. Its doctrines are holy, its precepts are binding, its histories are true, and its decisions are immutable. Read it to be wise, believe it to be safe, and practice it to be holy. It*

contains light to direct you, food to support you, and comfort to cheer you. It is the traveler's map, the pilgrim's staff, the pilot's compass, the soldier's sword, and the Christian's charter. Here too, Heaven is opened, and the gates of Hell disclosed. Christ is its grand subject, our good its design, and the glory of God its end. It should fill the memory, rule the heart, and guide the feet. Read it slowly, frequently and prayerfully. It is a mine of wealth, a paradise of glory, and a river of pleasure. It is given to you in life, will be opened at the judgment, and be remembered forever. It involves the highest responsibility, rewards the greatest labor, and will condemn all who trifle with its sacred contents."

Every time I read that, I get chills all over again because I know that the Word of God will absolutely change and transform our lives in a way that is very difficult to describe. There are very few things in the world that will make a difference, even close to what the word of God does. When you trust God, your focus is on him, not your problem. You also must understand that it's very easy to get frustrated if you stay in a position of constantly thinking about the problem instead of the answer. Remember that there is nothing wrong with thinking about things, planning, organizing, and structuring things that work out to your benefit. That is not where the problem is. The problem is in overthinking, over-preparing, over-organizing, and over-structuring to the point that you cannot possibly maintain all these things. **Earlier in this book, I used the term paralysis by analysis, and that's exactly what overthinking leads to.** You can get to the place where you have so many moving parts and spinning plates that it is impossible to keep up. And then, if you add some negativity to that, some time pressure, a couple of kids yelling at you, and a dog barking at you, before you know it, you have a real mess! Again, the people who are happy-go-lucky in life may not even face these same pressures, fears, or uncertainties, but it can be easy for you! Most people around you will not understand you overthinking things and will never see it the same way you do. That alone can be very frustrating, especially when it involves people that you love and people who are close to you. It is a difficult thing to not really be able to explain your situation to others because you know they just won't get it.

"Fear is only as strong as your mind
allows it to be."
—unknown

5

The "What If" Game

To an organized and very prepared person, playing the "what if" game can easily become a habitual pattern. I know what you might be saying to yourself; "Organized? Prepared? — Well, count me in!" Organized and prepared people tend to be scenario-based thinkers. It is great to be organized and prepared, but when the preparation and the planning are taken to an extraordinary level, people like this can be left seeking answers that are simply not attainable.

Playing the "what if" game keeps us stuck in a perpetual cycle of fear.

The "what if" game sounds something like this: "I do not like flying because what if the plane goes down? I will never eat there again, because the last time I ate there I got sick, and what if that happens again? I don't want to go to that party because what if I don't know anyone there? I could never ask for a salary increase because what if they simply say no? I really don't want to cross that long bridge because what if it is not built strong enough and it falls? We have to go back to the house because what if I forgot and left the stove turned on? The iron on? The garden hose on?" And on and on it goes, where it stops, nobody knows!

Playing the "what if" game keeps us stuck in a perpetual cycle of fear. It consumes our thoughts and occupies our minds, leaving little room for positive or constructive thinking. Every moment is spent concentrating on the negative possibilities, creating a constant state of anxiety and worry. The game offers no respite; it is a relentless and never-ending stream of thoughts and scenarios. What's even worse is that one negative thought often leads to another, creating a domino effect that intensifies fear and magnifies the perceived risks. It is a dangerous trap that keeps us stuck in fear. To play this game is to walk in fear constantly.

This fear-driven mindset has severe consequences for our personal growth and overall well-being. It hinders our progress by paralyzing us with over-analysis, preventing us from acting and seizing opportunities. The constant focus on potential negative outcomes stifles our potential, keeping us confined within the boundaries of our comfort zones. As a result, we miss out on valuable experiences, personal growth, and the realization of our true potential.

Additionally, playing the "what if" game robs us of the joy and freedom that God intends for us to experience. Instead of embracing life with trust, confidence, and faith, we become trapped in a cycle of fear and limitation. Our minds are consumed by the negative, overshadowing the beauty and abundance of God's blessings. This constant dwelling on hypothetical scenarios robs us of the peace and contentment that come from living in the present moment and trusting in God's providence.

The "what if" game perpetuates a distorted view of reality. By focusing solely on the negative possibilities, we become detached from the truth and lose sight of God's faithfulness and goodness. It breeds a mindset of doubt and skepticism, undermining our ability to trust in God's plan and provision. As a result, we may become more susceptible to the enemy's lies and deception, further deepening our fears and anxieties.

Breaking free from the grip of the "what if" game requires a shift in our mindset and a renewed perspective. We must intentionally choose faith over fear, trust over doubt, and gratitude over worry. By anchoring ourselves in the truth of God's Word and seeking His guidance, we can break free from this destructive pattern and embrace a life of peace, joy, and freedom.

In the following pages, we will explore in greater detail the detrimental effects of playing the "what if" game. We will delve into the psychological and emotional toll it takes on individuals, as well as its impact on relationships, decision-making, and overall well-being. We will uncover the lies that fuel this fear-driven mindset and discover practical strategies and biblical truths to overcome its grip. By the end, we will be equipped with the tools to break free from the bondage of fear and live fully in the abundant life that God intends for us.

Let us take a moment to explore the dangers of playing the "what if" game and how to use the power of God's Word to overcome this fear. For the sake of simplicity, let us talk about several specific and unique elements included in the "what if" game.

Paralysis by Analysis

When we engage in the "what if" game, we tend to overanalyze every possible scenario, weighing risks and uncertainties excessively. This analysis paralysis keeps us trapped in a state of inaction, inhibiting our growth, and preventing us from stepping into new opportunities. Proverbs 3:5-6 reminds us to trust in the Lord, acknowledge His guidance, and surrender our understanding to Him. By letting go of the need for complete control, we open ourselves to God's wisdom and His straight path for our lives.

Wasted Energy and Time

Playing the "what if" game consumes our mental and emotional energy, leading to unnecessary stress and anxiety. It robs us of the peace and contentment that God desires for us. Matthew 6:27 teaches us the futility of worry, reminding us that being anxious cannot add a single hour to our lives. Instead of expending our energy on fear, we can redirect it toward seeking God's kingdom and His righteousness, trusting that He will provide for our needs.

The fear-driven mindset of the "what if" game often leads to missed opportunities for growth, joy, and blessing. It holds us back from taking risks, trying new things, and stepping out of our comfort zones. Ecclesiastes 11:4 encourages us to embrace a mindset of faith and action, urging us not to be paralyzed by observing the wind or regarding the clouds. Instead, we are called to sow seeds of faith, trusting that God will bring forth a bountiful harvest.

Lack of Trust in God

Constantly playing the "what if" game reveals a lack of trust in God. But Romans 8:28 assures us that all things work together for the good of those who love God and are called according to His purpose. **By surrendering our fears and anxieties to Him, we can find comfort in knowing that He is in control.** We can trust that even in challenging circumstances, He has a plan and will work everything for our ultimate good.

Limited Faith and Growth

The "what if" game limits our faith in God's ability to provide, protect, and guide us. It hinders our spiritual growth and prevents us from experiencing the fullness of God's blessings. Hebrews 11:6 emphasizes the importance of faith, stating that without it, it is impossible to please God. By stepping out in faith, we open ourselves to God's transformative work in our lives and unlock the doors to His abundant blessings.

Self-Fulfilling Prophecies

When we constantly focus on negative "what if" scenarios, we inadvertently attract and manifest those very outcomes. Proverbs 23:7 emphasizes the power of our thoughts, revealing that as we think in our hearts, so we become. By renewing our minds with

God's truth and focusing on His promises, we can reshape our thinking patterns and cultivate a positive, faith-filled mindset.

Stagnation and Regret

The "what if" game keeps us stagnant, limiting our personal and spiritual growth. As a result, we may look back on our lives with regret, realizing that fear dictated our choices and caused us to miss out on countless opportunities. Philippians 3:13-14 encourages us to press on toward the goal, letting go of past regrets and straining forward to what lies ahead. By releasing the grip of fear, we can embrace the abundant life that God has in store for us.

If you are a highly organized and detail-oriented person, it can be easy to pride yourself on being prepared for every situation. The downside is that this trait will gradually transform your obsession into fear. For example, if you are planning a trip, making a major life decision, or even attending a social gathering, it can be easy to spend countless hours contemplating all the potential negative outcomes. This is exactly what I did for many years.

You could meticulously research every aspect of the trip, spend hours reading online reviews, analyzing weather patterns, and considering all the worst-case scenarios. What if the hotel had poor service? What if the flights were delayed or canceled? What if there is a natural disaster? These kinds of thoughts can completely consume your mind to the point where the joy of anticipation is overshadowed by anxiety and worry. This is the way I lived my life for so many years, but no longer!

By releasing the grip of fear,
we can embrace the abundant life
that God has in store for us.

The constant analysis leads to a lack of spontaneity and an inability to fully enjoy the present moment. You can become so caught up in the "what if" scenarios that it impacts your relationships and limits your experiences. This fear-driven mindset will hinder you from embracing the beauty and adventure of life. Sometimes, it is not until you really recognize the toll it takes on you that you choose to finally let go of excessive planning and worry and begin to experience the freedom and peace that you deserve. I know that may sound a bit harsh, but you have to start somewhere.

Part of the reason that I can write about these things so candidly is because I have lived this in my own life. I have been hindered in life by this very kind of thinking, and it is horrible. It is one of the reasons that I have chosen to write this book. My aim is to potentially help other people avoid the pitfalls that come with this kind of negative thinking. Again, I think it is great to think about things, to have a plan, and to be an organized person in life. There is no problem with that. The problem is when things are taken to excess! When this kind of thinking occupies your entire life. That is when it becomes dangerous and harmful. Not only to you but to those around you, too.

You could be an ambitious entrepreneur with big dreams. But you can let the fear of failure hold you back from taking risks and pursuing your passions. Every time you consider a new business opportunity, your mind is flooded with doubts and negative scenarios. For instance, when presented with an opportunity to start your own company, you could find yourself paralyzed by thoughts of potential failure. What if you invested your time and resources only to see the business crumble? What if you faced financial ruin and embarrassment? These thoughts can consume your mind, leading you to hesitate and miss out on potentially life-changing opportunities.

This fear-driven mindset limits your growth and keeps you inside a comfort zone. If you can recognize the detrimental impact fear is having on your life, then you can break free from its grip. With the support of loved ones and a renewed sense of faith, you can gradually begin to challenge the negative thought patterns and embrace a mindset of courage and trust in God's provision. As you take steps forward, even in the face of uncertainty, you will discover joy and fulfillment, experiencing the truth that growth and success often come through stepping outside of your comfort zone.

Situations like these serve as reminders of how the "what if" game can impact the various aspects of our lives. From planning vacations to pursuing dreams, fear-driven thinking can hinder our progress, rob us of joy, and limit our personal growth. It is up to us to recognize these patterns and intentionally choose faith over fear to break free from its grip and begin living a life that is marked by freedom and peace.

Anchoring ourselves in the truth of God's Word and surrendering our fears to Him allows us to finally break free from this dangerous trap. We can have a mindset of faith. Here are some additional Scriptures that will encourage you.

- Psalm 56:3: "When I am afraid, I put my trust in you."

- Isaiah 41:10: "Fear not, for I am with you; be not dismayed, for I am your God; I will strengthen you, I will help you, I will uphold you with my righteous right hand."

- Matthew 6:34: "Therefore do not be anxious about tomorrow, for tomorrow will be anxious for itself. Sufficient for the day is its own trouble."

- Philippians 4:6-7: "Do not be anxious about anything, but in everything by prayer and supplication with thanksgiving let your requests be made known to God. And the peace of God, which surpasses all understanding, will guard your hearts and your minds in Christ Jesus."

"Fear is the thief of dreams."
—Brian Krans

6

Fear vs. Perfect Love

First John 4:18 says, "There is no fear in love, but perfect love casts out fear. For fear has to do with punishment, and whoever fears has not been perfected in love." Now, listen to that same verse from The Passion Translation — "Love never brings fear, for fear is always related to punishment. But love's perfection drives the fear of punishment far from our hearts. Whoever walks constantly afraid of punishment has not reached love's perfection."

Fear and perfect love stand as opposing forces, each one vying for control over our lives. Fear works like a relentless oppressor, seeking to trip us up, suffocating our potential, and robbing us of joy. On the other hand, perfect love is a liberating power that wants to set us free from the chains of fear and lead us into a life of abundance.

I was born in the mid-1960s in Florida and spent my first 18 years there hiking and snorkeling and exploring some of the heavily wooded areas. Those were my stomping grounds! I was also well into my fear journey at that time and had a constant fear of being bitten by a snake while I was out in the woods. Not that anyone really wants to be bitten by a snake, but for me, it was a major fear. I think one of the only things that kept me going and kept me exploring in the woods was that I truly believed that if I was bitten, I could somehow get to a hospital, and they would have an antidote for the snakebite. I believe it is called an anti-venom that counteracts the poisonous venom of the snake. I was always fascinated with the fact that there was some type of antidote that would reverse the process of something else. In much the same way, God's perfect love is the antidote to fear's grip. When fear raises its ugly head and tries to bite you and inject you with its venom, the perfect love of God is just waiting to counteract that poison. But just like I planned to make my way to the hospital and get that antidote, it takes a little effort on your part to engage the antidote. Even though the antidote is sitting there, waiting, we still have to choose to use it.

When fear and perfect love collide, a profound inner battle begins. The entangled emotions of doubt and faith clash inside us, with fear demanding our surrender and perfect love inviting us to trust. It is in these moments of choice that we must take courage, drawing upon the faith we have within us.

When we truly grasp the depth and magnitude of God's love, fear loses its power over us

---

God's perfect love has the extraordinary power to cast out fear, offering us freedom, security, and peace during life's uncertainties. Since fear is a universal human experience, it tends to manifest in various forms and try to infiltrate every aspect of our lives. It can arise from past traumas, worries about the future, concerns about our worthiness, or even the unknown. Fear can stop us in our tracks, put a lid on our potential, and cancel our relationships. Fear attempts to steal our joy and cast a dark shadow on the true-life God has designed for us.

However, perfect love stands as this amazing antidote to that very same fear. God's love is not ordinary or conditional; it is perfect, unwavering, and all-encompassing. It emanates from the very essence of God's character and is freely made available to everyone. When we truly grasp the depth and magnitude of God's love, fear loses its power over us.

To comprehend the profound impact of perfect love on our fears, we must first understand the nature of fear and the transformative nature of God's love.

I am very aware that I opened this chapter quoting a verse from the New Testament, but it is such a powerful verse that it bears repeating. The Apostle John so beautifully captures the essence of perfect love casting out fear in 1 John 4:18, where he writes, "There is no fear in love, but perfect love casts out fear. For fear has to do with punishment, and whoever fears has not been perfected in love."

So, let's unpack this verse a little bit and take a closer look at how it actually works!

Perfect love and fear cannot coexist. They are incompatible and mutually exclusive. In the presence of perfect love, fear diminishes and loses its grip on our hearts and minds. God's love is not tainted with fear or insecurity; it is complete, unblemished, and all-sufficient. In almost the exact same way, light stands in total contradiction to darkness. That is easy to understand, isn't it? If you have ever stood in a completely dark room and then turned on a light, you know that darkness immediately goes away in the presence of light. Because they stand in direct opposition to each other. Well, God's love is light, and fear is darkness! Light is stronger than darkness, so the moment light comes on the scene, darkness goes. I have always loved a particular section of scripture in the New Testament. In the first few verses of First John, the Apostle John describes many things that he and his fellow disciples experienced while they were with Jesus. He talks about the things that they all heard about and things they all saw with their own eyes. They physically walked and talked with Jesus. He says it like this: 1 John 1:1-4 "That which was from the beginning, which we have heard, which we have seen with our eyes, which we looked upon and have touched with our hands, concerning the word of life — the life was made manifest, and we have seen it, and testify to it and proclaim to you the eternal life, which was with the Father and was made manifest to us — that which we have seen and heard we proclaim also to you, so that you too may have fellowship with us; and indeed our fellowship is with the Father and with his Son Jesus Christ. And we are writing these things so that our joy may be complete." Verse five is where it starts to shape up! Verse five says, "This is the message we have heard from Him and proclaim to you, that God is light, and in Him is no darkness at all." Wow! I think that is amazing. Of all the things that John could have written about here, of all the things he saw and experienced by walking daily with Jesus Himself, John chose to write about light. John knew the secret. He understood that in the Light of God's love, demonstrated by sending His only Son Jesus, darkness had to completely flee. Darkness had no choice in the matter! Perfect light casts out darkness, and perfect love casts out fear! I just love that.

Remember that fear has to do with punishment, and whoever fears has not been perfected in love. According to this verse, fear is closely tied to the idea of punishment. It arises from a sense of guilt, shame, or a belief that we will face negative consequences. However, in Christ, we find redemption and forgiveness. Through His sacrifice, Jesus already took the punishment for our sins, removing the need for fear. Did you hear what I just said? You do not need to fear! As recipients of God's perfect love, we are no longer under condemnation or punishment.

The Greek word that was translated as "no" in this verse is "ou" and is the absolute negative for the word "no." This means there is zero fear in God's kind of love. If we are experiencing fear, we are not experiencing God's love perfectly or completely. God's perfect love removes all fear.

The King James version of this verse states that "fear has torment." Fear torments. Those who serve God out of fear serve God out of torment. That will not work for long. Many people turn away from God not because they do not believe He exists but because they have been taught to serve God out of fear of punishment, and they are tormented. So, to escape the torment, they turn away from God. If they just knew the perfect love of God for them, in spite of their sins, they would turn back to the Lord.

If there is perfect or complete love, then there must be imperfect or incomplete love. Only perfect love casts out fear. If we still fear the Lord's punishment or lack of intervention on our part, our love is not perfect. We need the help of the Holy Spirit to explore the height, depth, length, and breadth of God's love, according to Ephesians 3:14-19 which says, "For this reason I bow my knees before the Father, from whom every family in heaven and on earth is named, that according to the riches of his glory he may grant you to be strengthened with power through his Spirit in your inner being, so that Christ may dwell in your hearts through faith—that you, being rooted and grounded in love, may have strength to comprehend with all the saints what is the breadth and length and height and depth, and to know the love of Christ that surpasses knowledge, that you may be filled with all the fullness of God." That is a mouthful! Perfect love will transform you. It has the power to heal wounds, restore brokenness, and cast out fear. When we experience the depth of God's love, it changes us from within. It reshapes our perspective, realigns our priorities, and infuses us with confidence, knowing that we are unconditionally loved by the Creator of the universe.

Those who still experience fear have not yet been perfected in love. The journey to overcoming fear involves growing in our understanding and experience of God's love. It is a process of deepening our relationship with Him, allowing His love to penetrate every aspect of our being.

To fully grasp the power of perfect love casting out fear, we must immerse ourselves in the truths of Scripture and develop an intimate relationship with God. As we meditate on His promises and abide in His love, fear completely loses its grip on our lives.

Consider the following Scriptures that further emphasize the nature of God's perfect love:

- Romans 8:38-39 "For I am sure that neither death nor life, nor angels nor rulers, nor things present nor things to come, nor powers, nor height nor depth, nor anything else in all creation, will be able to separate us from the love of God in Christ Jesus our Lord."

- 1 John 4:16 "So we have come to know and to believe the love that God has for us. God is love, and anyone who abides in love abides in God, and God abides in them."

- Ephesians 3:17-19 "So that Christ may dwell in your hearts through faith—that you, being rooted and grounded in love, may have strength to comprehend with all the saints what is the breadth and length and height and depth, and to know the love of Christ that surpasses knowledge, that you may be filled with all the fullness of God."

As we allow the truth of God's Word and His perfect love to permeate our hearts, fear gradually loses its power. We learn to trust in His unfailing love, finding security and peace even in the face of uncertainty.

Perfect love, which originates from God, has this amazing ability to rid you of fear, but we have to let it! When we understand and embrace the His love, fear loses its grip on our lives. Through Christ's sacrifice, we are no longer under condemnation but rather recipients of His great love. As we grow in our knowledge and experience of God's love, fear diminishes, and we find freedom, peace, and joy in the presence of the One who loves us unconditionally.

> *"Fear is a reaction. Courage is a decision."*
> —*Winston Churchill*

7

The Voice and Result of Fear

If my wife calls me on my phone, I can immediately recognize her voice, just as you would expect. Even if I don't look at my phone first to see that she is the one calling, I can still tell it is her. The reason for that is I have spent a great deal of time with her over the years and have heard her voice many, many times. I am quite used to the sound of her voice and the kind of things that she may say. She has a certain quality and tone in her voice that makes it very easy for me to recognize. I am sure this story is repeated over and over in your life, too, with your family and friends. I am not only familiar with the tone of her voice but also what she says. It would be completely out of character for my wife to say something harsh or edgy because she already has a long track record of being a very pleasant and sweet person who only says nice things. *(If you have not been keeping track, I am hoping to score some major brownie points right there! — Love you, honey!)*

Well, fear has a certain voice, too. It has a certain sound to it. To truly talk about freedom from fear and anxiety, I think it is helpful to understand what that voice sounds like and the kinds of things that it says. The reason for this is that it is important to recognize what fear looks like and what voice it uses. If you do not recognize what fear sounds like and looks like, you stand a good chance of continuing to walk in it daily. You need to completely understand that fear brings with it some very devastating consequences. Hopefully, this will light a fire under you, causing you to do something about your situation and rid yourself of fear and anxiety. Obviously, fear and anxiety are terrible, but I do not just want you to take my word for it; why don't we also look at some scientific proof?

The University of Minnesota has continued to conduct studies by the Earl E. Bakken Center for Spirituality & Healing. In their ongoing research, they have studied the impact of fear and anxiety, how fear works, how fear impacts our thinking, and many other related subjects. There are studies that have shown that when people live in constant fear, whether from physical dangers in their environment or threats they perceive, they can experience negative impacts in all areas of their lives and even become incapacitated. They also indicate that fear prepares us to react to danger. Once we sense a potential danger, our body releases hormones that slow or shut down functions not needed for survival, such as our digestive system. It also sharpens functions that might help us survive, such as eyesight. Our heart rate increases and blood flows to our muscles so we can run faster.

The brain reacts immediately to signals from the amygdala instead of more rational processing. The amygdala is a part of the brain used to perform a primary role in the processing of memory, decision-making, and emotional responses, including fear, anxiety, and aggression. When in this overactive state, the brain perceives events as negative and remembers them that way. The brain then stores all the details surrounding the danger. The sights, sounds, odors, time of day, weather, and so forth. These memories tend to be very durable, although they may also be fragmented. The details of these events can trigger fear later and bring back the memory, or they may cause us to feel afraid without consciously knowing why. Because these cues were associated with previous danger, the brain may see them as a predictor of threat. In some cases, this can result in post-traumatic stress disorder (PTSD). For example, a soldier who experienced a bombing on a foggy day might find himself panicking when the weather turns foggy—without knowing why.

The study goes on to show that living under this constant threat has serious health consequences. Fear weakens our immune system and can cause cardiovascular damage, gastrointestinal problems such as ulcers and irritable bowel syndrome, and decreased fertility. It can lead to accelerated aging and even premature death.

Fear can impair the formation of long-term memories and cause damage to certain parts of the brain, such as the hippocampus. This can make it even more difficult to regulate fear and can leave a person anxious most of the time. To someone in chronic fear, the world looks scary, and their memories confirm that.

Fear can also interrupt processes in our brains that allow us to regulate emotions, read non-verbal cues and other information presented to us, reflect before acting, and act ethically. This impacts our thinking and decision-making in negative ways, leaving us susceptible to intense emotions and impulsive reactions. All these effects can leave us unable to act appropriately.

Now, the last thing in the world that I want you to do is to get worried or concerned about what you just read! Keep in mind that this chapter is talking about "the results of fear." We are simply taking a closer look at what happens if we remain in fear and do not pursue a solution. It is also important to note that you are currently embarking on a mission to rid yourself of fear. That is exactly why you are reading this book right now. You are making positive steps in the right direction to remove fear and anxiety from your life, and that is great news! So, don't get too distracted by the scientific studies done by the University of Minnesota. God is much bigger than fear and anxiety, and he has provided a way out for you. Ok, now that we have taken a short break from scientific study, let's jump right back into this chapter and finish this up.

When fear assumes control, its terrible influence spreads like a toxic vine, strangling every aspect of our lives. It infiltrates our thoughts, poisoning our perceptions and distorting our reality. It is like virtual reality from the pit of hell. Its grip tightens, constricting our actions, stifling our dreams, and ultimately leading us down a treacherous path of despair and missed opportunities.

*When fear assumes control,
its terrible influence spreads like a toxic vine,
strangling every aspect of our lives.*

As fear takes root, it paralyzes us, rendering us powerless to break free from its suffocating grasp. It brings self-doubt, eroding our confidence and sabotaging us internally. Fear convinces us that we are inadequate, unworthy, and incapable of overcoming the things we face. It engulfs us in a state of perpetual anxiety, robbing us of peace and joy.

Fear governs our decisions, forcing us into the confines of our comfort zones. It erects walls, barricading us from new experiences and hindering our personal development. It whispers cautionary tales of failure and rejection, deterring us from pursuing our passions and realizing our true potential. Fear restricts our possibilities and traps us in a cycle of stagnation. Fear infiltrates our personal lives, poisoning the relationships we hold dear. It breeds suspicion, jealousy, and possessiveness. It corrodes the foundations of trust. Fear hampers our ability to connect authentically, building emotional barriers that impede intimacy and vulnerability. It distorts our perceptions of others, causing us to view them through a lens of doubt and skepticism.

Fear cripples our physical and mental health, inflicting a host of detrimental effects. It manifests as stress, wreaking havoc on our bodies and minds. The constant state of fight or flight consumes our energy, leaving us drained and susceptible to illness. Fear hampers our ability to sleep peacefully, impairing our cognitive function and diminishing our overall well-being.

The consequences of fear extend well beyond our individual lives, reaching out to our communities and society at large. Fear fuels division, animosity, and prejudice, fostering an environment of hostility and mistrust.

The terrible results of fear dominating our lives are far-reaching and profound. They deprive us of the richness and beauty that life has to offer. They keep us imprisoned in a state of perpetual anguish, preventing us from experiencing true freedom and fulfillment.

However, it is crucial to remember that God has given us the ability within us to break free from fear's grip. We have the capacity to cultivate courage, resilience, and faith. By embracing love, hope, and trust, we can dismantle fear's dominion entirely.

I remember, on a couple of occasions, having to go to the emergency room because I thought I was having a heart attack. In addition to going to the emergency room, I have also experienced what it is like to just go in for a regular doctor's check-up and describe some of the symptoms that I was experiencing in my body. In each case, I did not have a heart attack at all. Each time, the doctors did a full examination of my heart, drew blood, took my blood pressure, and did all the normal things that a doctor would do to determine what was going on with me. Once it was discovered that I was not in serious danger, then came the obvious questions. If I am not having some major attack in my body, what is happening in my body that makes me feel this way? For me personally, each time I experienced those symptoms, my doctor looked at me and told me that I was absolutely stressed out to the max. And then, of course, they would ask me what I did for a living, hoping to find the source of the anxiety and stress. Once I let them know that I was in full-time ministry, that opened a whole new set of questions! Isn't that something? Here I am, working full-time in the ministry, supposedly working in a field that should be the most peaceful and the most enjoyable, and yet I was stressed out to the max.

It was not until many years later that I started understanding that fear is not something that is done to you; it is something you accept, take, and believe. There are many people all around you in your life who can do things to you, say things to you, and even create an atmosphere of stress and anxiety all around you. But ultimately, it is up to you and me to accept what has been done and receive it. Again, anxiety is not necessarily caused by what someone has done to you, but it is caused when you receive it. Although it can easily be explained away that someone has done something to you that has caused you to walk in fear and anxiety, it is simply not true! Do you remember earlier in the book when we were talking about the "let switch?" Do you remember that Bible verse that stated that we are to "let not our hearts be troubled?" The bottom line is that we receive these sensations in our physical body because of the anxieties and fears that we take on ourselves. It is not someone else's fault that we feel this way; it is something we have done to ourselves. Most of the time, this happens because of a lack of knowledge. We simply do not understand what we are doing. If we understood the process of receiving stress and anxiety, none of us would ever take it. So, let us be about the business of educating ourselves, gaining a much clearer understanding of how this works, and once and for all, stop receiving fear and anxiety from certain situations.

Fear is imaginary. Fear is fake, but we make it real when we take it into our minds and our bodies, and we let it have free reign inside of us. That is where the real danger begins. Fear may be present, but you have to open the present! If you can accept fear, you can also reject fear. The real question becomes, is there really an end to fear and anxiety? Well, it just so happens that the title of the very next chapter in this book is "Will It Ever End?" Trust me, help is on the way!

Fear is imaginary. Fear is fake,
but we make it real when we take it into our minds
and our bodies, and we let it have free reign inside of us.

"Fear is only as deep as the mind allows."
—Japanese Proverb

8

Will It Ever End?

Anytime you start talking about fear, inevitably, the nagging question arises: "Will it ever end?" Is there really any end in sight, or are we seriously just stuck here on a journey going nowhere? It is easy to find ourselves entangled in the clutches of anxiety, uncertainty, and doubt, yearning for a glimmer of hope or a sign that freedom is on the horizon. As we begin this chapter, it is vital to have a sense of hope, for it is hope that illuminates the path ahead and assures us that the reign of fear is not eternal.

Hope is a profound force that goes way beyond our circumstances and speaks to the very core of our being. Having hope will affirm that fear is not an all-encompassing reality but rather a temporary visitor in our lives.

When fear overwhelms us, it often feels all-consuming, as if its grip will never be loosened. Fear whispers lies, attempting to convince us that some terrible thing is inevitable and inescapable. But hope reminds us of the short-lived nature of fear. It gently prompts us to look beyond the present moment to a future where fear's power is eradicated. There are times that it seems like fear is continually crashing upon us, and it may attempt to convince us that it will be with us forever, but hope reminds us to believe otherwise. Hope chooses to see the truth that fear is just a passing visitor, one that can be acknowledged, confronted, and ultimately overcome.

Hope stirs within us a sense of anticipation. It sees the seeds of possibility, reminding us that fear is not absolute. Hope turns the tables on fear so that it is hope that becomes our constant companion instead of fear. So, as we journey through life, hope strengthens our resolve and reminds us that, even in the darkest of times, a new day is on the horizon.

Hope chooses to see the truth that fear is just a passing visitor, one that can be acknowledged, confronted, and ultimately overcome.

While fear may try to persist, hope reminds us that it is not invincible. It acknowledges the weight of our fears, and yet it steadfastly believes in change. God does not want any of us to be fearful or afraid. But he does want us to have a healthy respect and reverence for the things of God. God's desire is that you lack no good thing, and he will help each step of the way. Knowing He is with you, knowing that He has a plan for your life, you can be confident that He will lead you through it; you have no need to fear.

Psalm 23:4-6 "Even though I walk through the darkest valley, I will fear no evil, for you are with me; your rod and your staff, they comfort me. You prepare a table before me in the presence of my enemies. You anoint my head with oil, my cup overflows. Surely your goodness and love will follow me all the days of my life, and I will dwell in the house of the Lord forever."

The early church Christians faced many trials. They knew they were not alone, and that God was with them. They knew that there was nothing to fear, even when they faced death at times for their faith. In the midst of persecution, the church grew, and believers refused to submit to unhealthy fears because they trusted God with all their hearts.

Hope has a way of reminding us that fear cannot flourish when faith in Christ is present. Unhealthy fears do not lead to anything good, but a healthy fear and faith in God Almighty bring joy, hope, and the strength to persevere in trials and grow closer to God. So, if you find yourself experiencing a time when the enemy is whispering fear into your ear, just know that voice is not from God. You may experience ridicule or attacks of some kind from people because of your faith in Christ but simply refuse to shrink back. Trust the Lord. Know that He is with you, and nothing can separate you from Him as you walk in faith and victory. There may be spiritual attacks in the form of worldly trials but remember that Christ in you is your hope of Glory. Do not let opposition cause you to develop unhealthy fear. Remain steadfast in Christ. Remain focused on Jesus and ignore all the junk that the enemy wants you to focus on.

I want you to consider three powerful thoughts found in 2 Timothy 1:7. The thoughts are power, love, and sound mind.

Acts 1:8 tells us, "But you will receive power when the Holy Spirit comes on you, and you will be my witnesses in Jerusalem, and in all Judea and Samaria, and to the ends of the earth." The kind of power that God gives us does not allow room for unhealthy fear. When a believer has the Holy Spirit working in, and through them, there is nothing that cannot be accomplished that is in line with the will of God. We must take a stance against unhealthy fear and know beyond any doubt that God is with us. As we lean on the Lord and fulfill the plans of God that are in our hearts, we can be assured that we will succeed. If you begin to experience unhealthy fear, seek the Lord and do not allow the enemy to rob you or cause you to doubt. Seek the Lord and His will, and God will receive all the glory.

---

*We must take a stance against unhealthy fear
and know beyond any doubt
that God is with us.*

Again, in 1 John 4:18, we see, "There is no fear in love. But perfect love drives out fear, because fear has to do with punishment. The one who fears is not made perfect in love." When we walk in the spirit of Love, when we love as Christ loved us, we will not be bound by unhealthy fear. Perfect love drives out fear. Perfect love is healthy, and it strengthens our relationship with God and with others. When we love as Christ loves us, there is no need to fear, as we are walking in the love of God. Everything we do, we will do with the desire to please God, and we will honor and glorify God. This is an unconditional kind of love. It is considered the highest form of love. It is the love of God for man and of man for God.

The third idea is a sound mind or self-discipline. I can guess that we all may have struggled with self-discipline at one time or another. Having a sound mind involves self-discipline. It takes a sound mind to recognize unhealthy fear and then turn away from it. It takes a sound mind to remain faithful to God and not become distracted by the enemies' tricks and lies that he may bring to you.

The enemy may use a person or an advertisement, or you may overhear a conversation, and the seed of unhealthy fear can take root. Always be on alert. Those seeds of fear are rarely noticed. I believe that is why the apostle Paul wanted to remind young Timothy to remain faithful and keep the gift of God alive, and to burn bright for all to witness. This would take constant attention on Timothy's part to remain reliant on God. 2 Timothy 1:6-7 (NIV), "For this reason I remind you to fan into flame the gift of God, which is in you through the laying on of my hands. For the Spirit God gave us does not make us timid, but gives us power, love, and self-discipline." Just like Timothy, we are supposed to be fanning into flame the gift of God in our lives and allowing the unhealthy fears to melt away.

I did a lot of stupid things when I was a young boy, and arguably, I still do a lot of stupid things now. I used to really like to play with fire when I was growing up. Looking back on those times, I can see that it was a very unhealthy thing, but it sure was fun at the time. Just like the other boys in my small neighborhood, we all had a certain sense of curiosity. One day, I joined several other boys in an attempt to boil an egg. I had watched my mother many times boil an egg in a pan on the stove, and now it was my turn. Sure, it would have been easy to just put an egg in a pot on the stove, but there is no fun in that! Instead, all of us boys made our way out into a wooded area near where we lived. It was a dry Florida pine forest area adjacent to our neighborhood. We had decided that we would place an egg inside of a glass mayonnaise jar, fill the jar with water to the top, and then screw the lid on tight. The next steps would be to start a fire and place the jar in the middle of the fire, hoping to boil the water and the egg. As you can imagine, even if we had succeeded, the jar would have exploded, sending glass shards all through us. We never got the chance to find out, though, because the fire quickly got out of control. Did I mention that we were in the middle of a dry forest? Of course, we had started the fire by scooping a bunch of dry pine forest needles into a pile and lighting it on fire. Obviously, we did not anticipate what would happen next. We did not end up with the desired results that day, but what we did end up with was a forest fire. By the time the fire department arrived to put out the fire, it had consumed 27 acres of prime land in the middle of Florida. Fortunately for me, I was probably the youngest boy there and did not really get any of the blame that day. I did lose a very well-constructed wooden fort and two very nice tree houses! My life would never be the same! All of this happened because we decided to fan the flame. The flame ended up consuming everything around it, and we really were not thinking about much else while we were running for our lives. Fire tends to consume everything.

If we are to be the people of God that He desires and has called us to be, it will take us having a sound mind that is firmly focused on the Lord. It can only be done in the power of the

Holy Spirit, as the love of God rules in our hearts because of our faith in Christ. The process of developing a sound mind and living a life of faith where we have a healthy fear and reverence of the Lord is called sanctification, where we act and live as being set apart unto God. A person being conformed to the image of Christ is not a person who is bound by unhealthy fears. Rather, we have the spirit of power, love, and of self-discipline, and we do not fear life's trials and struggles.

I am sure you can attest that there are many different trials and adversities in life. Trials and adversities can cause you to shut down and incite unhealthy fears if you allow them. But understand that is not what God wants, nor is it from Him.

I am sure by now that you are beginning to understand that unhealthy fears are destructive and will steal your joy. They will keep you from physical and spiritual success and hold you back in every way in life. But, by keeping our hope firmly planted in God, we will be able to maintain the spirit of power, love, and a sound mind. It is this same hope in God that will give us the ability to say no to evil, avoid bad habits and worldly temptations, and consistently embrace God's love and goodness every day.

If you are having doubts about any of this, I encourage you to begin today by praying and asking the Lord to reveal to you the hope that you have in Christ. Make the effort to focus on Christ in every circumstance and not on worldly distractions. Decide to remain spiritually steadfast in the Word of God and allow the Holy Spirit to speak to you through that Word. And finally, begin to thank the Lord for the gift of God that is in your heart. Always remember that you are never alone. You are a child of God. He is with you, and He is preparing a table before you in the presence of your enemies (Psalm 23:5). You have no reason to fear as the world fears. God is with you.

9

A Brief Explanation

I would like to congratulate you on making it this far into the book. I know we have had to talk about some very difficult things. It is also important to understand that you are making good progress! I think I could even say that I am proud of you at this point for sticking with it. I also want you to know that hope is on the horizon! So far, we have been discussing the subject of fear, anxiety, and overthinking in a more general sense. A big change is about to happen in this book right now. We are about to move into some discussion about individual fears on a very specific level. This is where the rubber meets the road! This is where you will begin to see how certain fears have worked against you throughout your life and the damage that has come as a result.

The next 15 chapters are very different than all those prior. The following chapters are not very lengthy but rather meant as a reference point. I hope you'll read the chapters, use the information for your situation, make changes to be free, and keep the book handy for future reference. In the coming chapters, we will explore some detailed information regarding

15 specific fears we each face from time to time. We certainly cannot address every single fear that mankind faces each day, as there are already volumes of books written about those. So, rather than commenting on the fear of heights or spiders, we will look more closely at the kinds of fear that haunt us mentally and keep us from fulfilling God's purpose for us. I will let you deal with the spiders as you see fit!

So, we are going to confront these fears head-on, delving deep into their intricacies, unraveling their complexities, and unveiling strategies to overcome them. But before we embark on this mission, I challenge you to make sure that you keep a solid hope set out in front of you! You must steadfastly believe that the struggle against fear is not in vain and that you will ultimately come out on top! Remember that the journey toward freedom from fear is profound, requiring patience, self-compassion, and a steadfast commitment to change. What I am trying to say is that there is hope! I believe in you! You can do this! And no, I do not like heights or spiders either! Just ask my wife!

Each of the following chapters contains these sections:

1. The name of a specific fear.

2. A brief explanation of that fear.

3. The inherent dangers of that fear.

4. Scriptures related to that fear.

5. Steps you can take to overcome that fear.

Get ready for some serious progress!

"The key is to learn to trust God, no matter what our fears are. And we can trust Him because He loves us, and He is greater than anything we'll ever face."
—Billy Graham

10

Fear of Man

The fear of man can be a major hindrance to people from fulfilling their God-given purpose in life. This fear is rooted in the desire for other people's approval, acceptance, and validation. It focuses so much on pleasing someone else's wishes and desires that it completely incapacitates you. The whole aim of your life soon becomes making sure that you make all the right moves and say all the right things so that the person you are trying to please will not do something terrible to you. I know this sounds outrageous but remember that this is a mental battle. To walk in the fear of man is to be repeatedly controlled by someone else. The other person or people are squarely in charge of the outcome of every situation, and you are simply a pawn to fulfill what they want. The entire focus constantly stays on the other person and what you can do or say to keep their ongoing approval. We are not talking about sincere respect for someone at this point, but rather a genuine fear of that person, to the point that you will do, act, say, or think however they want you to, or else there will be some kind of swift and severe consequence.

Oftentimes, the controlling person does have the power to change something about your life, but in your mind, you can exaggerate this control and authority to ridiculous levels. Honestly, this was one of the main fears that I have had to deal with in my life personally. I had allowed other people and situations to dictate to me every move I made. I constantly felt like I was supposed to jump up and click my heels together whenever I was asked to, and sometimes even expected to act on things before I was asked. All the while, I had in the back of my mind that I would get severe negative results if I did not comply with every wish and desire. I know it is a horrible feeling to be controlled and manipulated by someone else. But again, keep in mind that most of the issue is not with the other person but in your mind. I even remember many occasions when my wife would try to console me by telling me that I was overthinking the situation and taking it way too far in my mind, but I could not see it. I could not get my mind wrapped around the fact that I had blown this up in my mind. I was making a mountain out of a molehill.

To walk in the fear of man is to be repeatedly controlled by someone else.

The fear of man is so detrimental. Unfortunately, I made the mistake of walking in the fear of man for so many years of my life. I can personally attest that this kind of fear is specifically designed to keep you from moving forward. The fear of man absolutely keeps you right where the other person or people want you.

The Danger of the Fear of Man is that it holds you captive, preventing you from embracing your true identity and living in freedom. Ultimately, it leads to compromise. You start to compromise your values, beliefs, and convictions to gain acceptance and approval from others. This is usually quickly followed by anxiety and insecurity and keeps you constantly worrying about others' opinions. All this does is rob you of peace and joy. This fear keeps you struggling to be genuine and transparent, wearing a mask to fit in and fearing rejection if your true self is ever revealed. It is all about a lack of authenticity. It can also hinder you from obeying God's calling and following His leading as you become more concerned with what people might think or say.

Here are some Scriptures to Consider:

- Proverbs 29:25 "The fear of man lays a snare, but whoever trusts in the Lord is safe."

- Galatians 1:10 "For am I now seeking the approval of man, or of God? Or am I trying to please man? If I were still trying to please man, I would not be a servant of Christ."

- Psalm 118:6 "The Lord is on my side; I will not fear. What can man do to me?"

- Matthew 10:28 "And do not fear those who kill the body but cannot kill the soul. Rather fear him who can destroy both soul and body in hell."

Overcoming the Fear of Man

The fear of man can be overcome through intentional steps and a deeper reliance on God. Put the focus back on God by shifting your attention from seeking man's approval to seeking God's approval. Remember that God's opinion of you is what truly matters. This is the time to embrace your identity in Christ and to understand that your worth and value come from being a child of God, not what others think of you. It is good to know your identity in Christ and find confidence in who He has created you to be. One of the easiest ways to do this is by simply meditating on God's Word as much as possible. Take the time to immerse yourself in the truth of God's Word. Meditate on scriptures that remind you of God's love, acceptance, and faithfulness. Learn to be genuine and transparent in your relationship with God too. You can tell Him anything and talk to Him about everything! Surround yourself with people who accept and support you for who you are. It is time to really trust in God and surrender all the control and outcomes to Him, knowing that He has a perfect plan for you.

You can also begin to take steps of faith and obedience to God, even when they may be uncomfortable or unpopular. Trust that God will provide the strength and courage you will need, no matter what you are facing. It is also good to stay accountable. Find a trusted mentor, counselor, or accountability partner who can support and encourage you in your journey to overcome the fear of man. By continually relying on God's strength, you can break free from the fear of man and live a life of authenticity, obedience, and freedom in Christ.

11

Fear of Premature Death

The fear of premature death is a gripping kind of fear that is based on how you think about things. So much of the time, this fear is completely based on things you have recently seen or heard. The kind of things that stay with you in your mind. At some point in time, practically everyone has had an aunt, or an uncle, a grandparent, or a friend die from some specific disease or ailment. And, of course, that ailment was undoubtedly surrounded by various symptoms. Then, one day, you have a similar symptom, and your brain automatically tells you that you must have that same disease or ailment that already caused their death. In fact, your mind contributes to believing that your situation is so similar that you will invariably die soon, even though there is no additional evidence to support it. It is a trick that your mind can play on you. The thing that makes it so believable is that most of the time, the concept of premature death is at least plausible. There are people who die prematurely. There are symptoms that those people may have had. In fact, if you live long enough, you will eventually die! But, in this chapter, we are not addressing whether or not you are going to die someday, but rather the fear that comes with believing it is just around the corner. The fear that constantly bombards you with thoughts that your time is up, that it is over, that there is no hope for you. But keep in mind that this fear typically bases all those thoughts on visual and audible cues that you have come across recently. The fact is that there is no real connection at all between your life and someone else who may have passed away prematurely. There is no real-world connection, and yet your mind tells you that if another person had this disease, you probably have it, too. Again, it is a trick. Once you begin to understand that this fear is a complete mind game, not based on reality at all, you will find that it is easy to overcome. We all like evidence. We all like facts. Well, turn this equation around and understand once and for all that the fear of premature death has absolutely no evidence or facts to back it up at all.

The fact is that there is no real connection at all between your life and someone else who may have passed away prematurely.

The Danger of the Fear of Premature Death is that it can have profound negative effects on you, constantly occupying space in your mind and using your valuable mental resources on a continuous basis. It is a complete waste of time! Soon enough, paralyzing anxiety: This fear leads to constant worry and anxiety, stealing away the joy and peace that sets in and begins to keep you from living in the present moment. You start to sit in stagnation and regret when you constantly consider dying before accomplishing your goals or dreams. It hinders you from ever taking risks, pursuing passions, and seizing opportunities, leading to a life filled with regret and unfulfilled potential. All this comes about because of a lack of trust in God's plan. This fear can cause you to doubt God's love for you and question His goodness, struggling to surrender your life fully into His hands. Constantly fearing premature death robs you of the ability to fully engage in relationships, experience new adventures, and savor the beauty and blessings of everyday life. It is the inability to embrace life!

Here are some Scriptures to Consider:

- Psalm 23:4 "Even though I walk through the valley of the shadow of death, I will fear no evil, for you are with me; your rod and your staff, they comfort me."

- Hebrews 2:14-15 "Since therefore the children share in flesh and blood, he himself likewise partook of the same things, that through death he might destroy the one who has the power of death, that is, the devil, and deliver all those who through fear of death were subject to lifelong slavery."

- Psalm 139:16 "Your eyes saw my unformed substance; in your book were written, every one of them, the days that were formed for me, when as yet there was none of them."

- John 11:25-26 "Jesus said to her, 'I am the resurrection and the life. Whoever believes in me, though he die, yet shall he live, and everyone who lives and believes in me shall never die. Do you believe this?'"

Overcoming the Fear of Premature Death

The fear of premature death can be overcome by a transformation of perspective and a deep trust in God's plan. Overcoming starts by learning to embrace God's love and acknowledge that God holds your life in His hands. Trusting in His perfect timing and divine plan for your days. Like many of these fears, it will always be important to learn to meditate on God's promises and build your life by surrounding yourself with scriptures that affirm God's presence, protection, and promise of eternal life. It is up to you to let these truths anchor your heart and mind. Instead of focusing on the fear of premature death, intentionally live each day with purpose and gratitude. Seize opportunities, cherish relationships, and pursue your passions with a sense of urgency and appreciation. You can also begin to cultivate a heavenly perspective, remembering that this life is not the end. Develop a perspective rooted in eternity, knowing that true life begins with Jesus and extends into eternity. Then you can begin to release your fears and anxieties into God's hands, surrendering your desire for control and entrusting your life to His loving care. You did not determine the day you were born, and you may not be able to determine the day you will ultimately die, but you can determine how you will live right now! Instead of continuously looking to the past, or casting doubt over your future, take the time to live in the present and make the most of the time that you have right now.

It is so important to also cultivate a vibrant relationship with God through prayer, worship, and studying His Word. Draw near to Him, and His peace will guard your heart and mind. The real turnaround can happen when you choose to replace fearful thoughts with faith-filled declarations. Speak God's promises over your life, declaring His protection, provision, and purpose. You can also begin to serve and impact others. When your focus shifts from self-preservation to making a difference in the lives of others, the fear of premature death suddenly loses its grip.

I am confident that if you will implement some of these basic strategies and continue to surround your fears with God, you will completely overcome this fear, and begin to live a purposeful life, knowing that your eternal destiny is secure in the hands of a loving and faithful God.

12

Fear of Failure

The fear of failure is a big fear for a lot of people. It is amazing how many people are walking around right now with no real hope for the future and an expectation that failure is just around the corner. This is a sad kind of fear. This is the kind of fear that just paralyzes people and prevents them completely from pursuing their dreams. The fear of failure is a dream stealer! This kind of fear prevents you from stepping out and doing what God has put in your heart to do. It completely prevents you from living to your full potential. The interesting thing about the fear of failure is that it tends to constantly put off or avoid any activity or scenario that even has the potential for an unsuccessful outcome. In other words, the fear of failure pre-determines your future without even giving you a chance to try. So, instead of reaching out and pursuing your dreams, you end up remaining scared to try new things, to take risks, or to even embrace growth of any kind. Oftentimes, the fear of failure is a close friend of procrastination, causing you to delay necessary tasks because you are uncertain about their outcome. In this way, a fear of failure makes it more difficult for someone to reach their goals because they are continuously put off into the future. It is a terrible thing to continuously worry that your plan, project, or goal will not succeed. I know, I've been there! This kind of failure also makes it difficult to make good decisions. Various symptoms of stress and anxiety may also accompany the fear of failure. These may very well include a faster heart rate, shallow breathing, sweating, and even muscle tension. You can usually tell that the fear of failure is close at hand when you begin feeling immediately afraid about the possibility of something failing, even if that task is easy, and the consequences of failure are very mild. If you find yourself continually avoiding all situations that could potentially fail, you are probably facing the fear of failure. This can also lead to difficulty in maintaining relationships, making progress in your career, or even participating in hobbies that you enjoy. Basically speaking, the fear of failure attempts to rob you of your future by painting a bleak picture of it on a continuous basis.

The fear of failure is a dream stealer!

The Danger of the Fear of Failure is that it can have profound negative effects on your life. It leads to missed opportunities. The fear of failure often leads to a reluctance to take risks and try new things. This keeps you from reaching out for growth, success, and personal development. This fear seems to target people who already have some degree of self-doubt or low esteem. This fear can erode self-confidence and self-worth, leading you to doubt your own abilities and potential. When you allow the fear of failure to control your actions, it restricts your ability to reach your goals, fulfill your purpose, and make a positive impact on the world. It literally limits your potential! When you give into the fear of failure, you will find that it results in a life filled with regret and unfulfilled dreams. It keeps you constantly looking back with a sense of what could have been.

Here are some Scriptures to Consider:

- Joshua 1:9 "Have I not commanded you? Be strong and courageous. Do not be frightened, and do not be dismayed, for the Lord your God is with you wherever you go."

- Philippians 4:13 "I can do all things through him who strengthens me."

- Psalm 37:23-24 "The steps of a man are established by the Lord, when he delights in his way; though he fall, he shall not be cast headlong, for the Lord upholds his hand."

- Romans 8:31 "What then shall we say to these things? If God is for us, who can be against us?"

Overcoming the Fear of Failure

To overcome the fear of failure, it is essential to shift your focus and mindset. It is important to embrace a new perspective rooted in faith and trust in God. Sometimes, we can actually hold the wrong definition of failure in our minds, so it may also be important to redefine what failure actually is and what it looks like. You should change your perspective of failure altogether. Instead, look at failure as an opportunity for growth, learning, and gaining valuable experience. Begin to take on the mindset that failure is simply a steppingstone to future success. Begin to shift your focus from success that is entirely outcome-based to one that includes the effort and growth that you put into your endeavors. Look at it as a way of continuously improving and celebrating your progress, regardless of the outcome. It is important to understand that your achievements or failures do not define your worth. So, embrace God's grace, knowing that His love and acceptance of you are not based on your performance.

Begin to replace negative and self-defeating thoughts with positive affirmations and God's promises. Meditate on scriptures that remind you of God's faithfulness, strength, guidance, and love. You might even want to challenge yourself to step out of your comfort zone and take some calculated risks. Trust that God is with you and will help you to overcome obstacles and achieve greatness. And you certainly can surround yourself with people who believe in you, encourage you, and provide a supportive community. Find some mentors and accountability partners who can offer guidance and wisdom along your journey. Please understand that setbacks and failures are part of life's journey. It is a good idea to develop some resilience and perseverance along the way, knowing that success often comes through perseverance in the face of obstacles.

A lot of the time, we look at success as something that we accomplish rather than seeking what God would like us to accomplish. Sometimes we are quick to put the emphasis on ourselves and not on God. I think it is very important to seek God's guidance and align your goals and dreams with His purpose for your life. When your pursuits are aligned with God's will, you can trust that He will equip and empower you to succeed. I also think that it is very helpful to view failures as opportunities for feedback and learning. Reflect on your experiences, identify areas for improvement, and adjust your approach accordingly.

If you could just bring yourself to implement some of these basic ideas and thoughts and learn to better trust God's guidance, you will be able to overcome the fear of failure and step into a life of boldness, growth, and purpose, knowing that your ultimate success is found in your obedience to God, rather than worldly standards of achievement.

13

Fear of Lack

If there was any fear that would work hand-in-hand with a fear of failure, it would most likely be the fear of lack. The fear of lack is a pervasive fear that revolves around the belief that there will never be enough. There will never be enough resources. There will never be enough provision. There will never be enough security. If you happen to be among those walking around, who have both the fear of failure and the fear of lack operating in your life, you have been given a double smack! When these two fears work together, not only will they convince you that you won't have enough, but they will also convince you that you are the reason that you will never have enough! That is no way to live life! You can easily tell if you are operating in the fear of lack if you constantly get the feeling that no matter what you do, there is never going to be enough. Not enough money, not enough time, not even enough energy to accomplish the things that you want to accomplish. Sometimes the fear of lack is deeply rooted in your past. If you grew up in a household that never really had much money and struggled to pay the bills all the time, you might take on the same thoughts that you also will never have enough and will always struggle to pay your bills.

The fear of lack will keep you from understanding that your future can be bright compared to those who came before you. The fear of lack often compares your experience to those around you who have much more. Once you go down that path, it is simply a comparison game for the rest of your life. Constantly basing what you have or don't have in relation or proportion to what someone else has or does not have. And I hate to say it, but even if you, or someone who has never really gone without, that doesn't necessarily stop you from worrying that someday you will. This kind of fear does not play fair. Again, like many of the other fears, it is not necessarily based on facts or reality but more on a negative mindset and a perspective view.

The fear of lack will keep you from understanding that your future can be bright compared to those who came before you.

The fear of lack tends to focus on the anxiety surrounding purchases or upcoming expenses, especially when those expenses are unexpected. The fear of lack causes you to worry about money and how you will be able to get things done. It's a constant feeling of frenzy which keeps you bouncing from one thing to the next. It is a constant attempt to fix things and make things right. Truthfully speaking, the fear of lack keeps the focus on yourself rather than others. It is a constant feeling and understanding that if you don't need the need, then it probably won't get met. Everything depends on you to come through, and if you come up short, that spells disaster and failure. So ultimately, you end up with the inability to enjoy the things that you do have because you are so focused on what you don't have. The fear of lack also keeps you constantly looking at what your friends and family have compared to what you have. This brings on feelings of jealousy toward them when they get something new, and you do not. It is mental competition, and mental comparing on a continuous basis.

Even as a believer in Christ, if you entertain the fear of lack, you will end up believing that God does provide – just not for me! It is a poverty or scarcity mindset that keeps you struggling all the time. Keep in mind that our current society is not helping you out here. The current culture that we see every day is absolutely bent on convincing you that you do not have the latest thing, you do not have enough money, you are not pretty enough, tall enough, tan enough, fast enough, educated enough, and all the other enoughs!

The Danger of the Fear of Lack is that it sets you up for unhealthy competition, jealousy, anxiety, overworking, and confusion about what really matters most. Ultimately, it leads to a scarcity mindset where you constantly dwell on what you lack rather than recognizing and appreciating the abundance you already have in your lives. Fear of lack breeds constant worry and anxiety about not having enough, leading to a state of perpetual stress and discontent. When you fear lack, you are often reluctant to give or bless others, fearing that you will lose what little you have left. The fear of lack can erode faith and trust in God's provision, leading you to rely solely on your own efforts and resources rather than seeking God's guidance and provision. The fear of lack is terrible. It only leads to more anxiety, worry, stifled generosity, hindered faith, and a lack of trust in God. It is no good at all!

Here are some Scriptures to Consider:

- Philippians 4:19 "And my God will supply every need of yours according to his riches in glory in Christ Jesus."

- Matthew 6:31-33 "Therefore do not be anxious, saying, 'What shall we eat?' or 'What shall we drink?' or 'What shall we wear?' For the Gentiles seek after all these things, and your heavenly Father knows that you need them all. But seek first the kingdom of God and his righteousness, and all these things will be added to you."

- Psalm 23:1 "The Lord is my shepherd; I shall not want."

- Luke 12:24 "Consider the ravens: they neither sow nor reap, they have neither storehouse nor barn, and yet God feeds them. Of how much more value are you than the birds!"

Overcoming the Fear of Lack

To break free from the fear of lack, it is vital to shift your perspective of abundance and trust in God's provision. Learn to walk with a heart of gratitude for the blessings and provisions you currently have. Focus on what you have rather than what you lack and become content with God's current provision for your life. It probably goes without saying, but I will say it anyway — Seek God's kingdom first! Prioritize seeking God's kingdom and His righteousness above all else. You may say that sounds too simple. It could be that you are overcomplicating things, too. Just think about it. Trust that as you align your life with His will, He will provide for your needs according to His abundant riches. Make it a point to purposely break free from the fear of lack by practicing generosity. Recognize that as you give and bless others, God's provision and abundance will flow into your life. Remind yourself of God's faithfulness throughout history and in your own life. Reflect on the ways He has provided for you in the past, and trust that He will continue to do so in the future. God has a pretty amazing track record.

*Prioritize seeking God's kingdom
and His righteousness above all else.*

Learn to release the grip of control and surrender your resources and provision to God. Trust that He is the ultimate provider and sustainer of your life. Also, seek God's wisdom in managing your resources and making financial decisions. Allow His guidance to lead you in stewarding what He has entrusted to you wisely. I think it is a good idea to challenge the fear of lack by stepping out in faith and giving generously. Trust that God will multiply your efforts and provide for your needs as you sow into His kingdom. Make sure that somewhere along the way, you also testify to someone else about how well God has provided for you in the past. Once again, this will keep the focus on what God has done instead of what you are currently facing. Give God credit for the great things he has done in your life. If you think about it for just a few minutes, you will realize the enormous efforts that God has already gone to for your provision. When you consider His tremendous track record of provision, it will be much easier for you to understand in your mind that God will continue to provide for you and supply everything that you need, according to His riches in glory, and not just what your bank account says.

These strategies will help you! I really encourage you to step out and trust God's provision. It is one of the primary ways that you are going to be able to break free from the fear of lack. You were destined by God to do great things for his kingdom, so now it is time to embrace a mindset of abundance, generosity, and faith, knowing that God is your ultimate source of that provision.

14

Fear of Not Being Good Enough

The fear of not being good enough is deeply rooted in the belief that your self-worth is either diminished or non-existent. This fear tends to hinder you by diverting your attention from your true identity in Christ. It is the obsessive fear of imperfection. Someone with this condition is simply terrified of making mistakes and tends to avoid any situation where they feel they will not succeed.

What does it even mean to feel "good enough?" How can you tell that someone else is good enough? What is so lacking about you that makes you not good enough? If you try to define "good enough," you will quickly realize that you are measuring yourself against a totally arbitrary standard. There is no real definition of "good enough" because your specific journey, experience, perspective, and approach are what will make you special. This is fantastic news because it means you cannot be anything other than "good enough."

The fear of not being good enough does not mean you are not good enough. You are probably just afraid because you have internalized feelings of self-doubt and self-criticism because of previous experiences you may have had. You dream big, and other people say your dreams are "unrealistic." It is when you are afraid to leave your comfort zone and use this fear as an excuse to avoid acting. But that is no excuse to stay stuck.

The truth is that when you feel you are not good enough, it is usually only compared to someone or something you see as better than you. It is a comparison game. The way this fear stops you in your tracks is by talking to you in your mind. It says things like, "You do not have enough experience. You are too young. You are too old. Your idea has already been used before. You are just trying to fool everyone. You will never get it perfectly, so you should not do it at all. You are a fraud, and everyone will figure it out soon enough. You are going to fail. You have too much to lose, so why even try?" Sound familiar? None of these messages are true. They are just reasons we give ourselves for feeling afraid and avoiding action. But you are good enough! Sometimes, you just need a reminder.

I remember so often feeling like I had to win the approval of other people all the time. It was a huge interruption in my life and caused me to be very negative all the time. Probably because I was constantly chasing after their approval instead of walking in who God already made me. It is an awful feeling to always be "behind." Always trying to catch up. I found myself having to go the extra mile all the time, always seeking and never attaining. I would not wish that fear on my worst enemies! It is terrible. I eventually had to have some help to break free of that mindset. Thank God someone helped me! That is exactly why this book means so much to me. I sincerely desire that this book be used as a tool to help others find their freedom from these fears. Fears are very real; they are not from God, and there is freedom beyond their grip.

When those "I'm not good enough" thoughts arise, notice them, then focus on what you want to achieve and who you are serving at that moment. When you turn your attention to helping others, you have no room to wonder whether you are good enough. When you worry that you are not good enough, you invite others to believe it, too. Before you assume your colleagues or your industry will not accept you, consider whether you have even accepted yourself first. Imagine yourself without fear. Identify the exact fear that's holding you back. Then, ask and answer this question: What would I create, attempt, or change about my life if the fear of failure or imperfection was not an issue?

When you turn your attention to helping others, you have no room to wonder whether you are good enough.

A big source of feeling like you are not being good enough is a fear of being judged. Don't assume people are judging you. When you assume people are standing by to attack, you will turbocharge those insecurities and focus too hard on what you think is not good enough about yourself. Just stop chasing approval! You have what it takes, and some people will simply never understand that. Stop measuring yourself against others' standards, and it will be much harder to convince yourself that you are not good enough. The comparison game is a trap. Enjoy your work and your life so much that your success cannot be questioned. It is tough for other people to judge you when you are already satisfied with your own results.

You know, you are amazing, and it is okay to have big dreams. You can move beyond self-sabotaging fears and pave the way to do that incredible work that only you can do.

The Danger of the Fear of Not Being Good Enough is that it creates self-doubt and insecurity in your mind. This often leads to constant questioning of your abilities, worth, and value. This quickly drives you to compare yourself to others, fostering feelings of inadequacy and jealousy as you strive to meet unattainable standards. Keep in mind that the fear of not being good enough is not limited to internal thoughts of inadequacy related to certain successes. It frequently has to do with your outward physical appearance, too. Even your status in life and what is perceived as your success. Our whole society is geared toward selling you the next product, and they will go to extreme levels of making you feel inadequate to sell you something that will bring you up to speed. They have attempted to create an urgency in you to become like someone you saw in the ad on TV or in that movie! But if you knew the flaws of all those perfectly tanned, beautiful people in the advertisements and movies, they would never even get your attention again. There is simply not enough surgery you can have, pills you can swallow, or acting classes you can take to get you to be like all the unrealistic, false presentations out there. Every picture of every man and every woman is manipulated to an unbelievable level using computer software. Many times, those models do not even end up with the original body parts but have someone else's eyes, lips, legs, or butt. Everything on them is stretched, toned, plumped, and distorted using graphic software. Those supermodels have been lifted, tucked, and puffed in all the right places just to give you the appearance that it is even attainable. It is not; in fact, it is not even real! Can you see how this fear works? Listen, God made you . . . You! He did not mess up when He made you, and if He had a second shot at making you again, He would do it again, exactly the way He did it to begin with!

The fear of not being good enough can paralyze you from pursuing your dreams and goals as you begin to believe you are not worthy or capable of success. If you are not cautious, you can struggle to accept and love yourself as you are, hindering personal growth and fulfillment.

Here are some Scriptures to Consider:

- Ephesians 2:10 "For we are his workmanship, created in Christ Jesus for good works, which God prepared beforehand, that we should walk in them."

- Psalm 139:14 "I praise you, for I am fearfully and wonderfully made. Wonderful are your works; my soul knows it very well."

- 2 Corinthians 12:9 "But he said to me, 'My grace is sufficient for you, for my power is made perfect in weakness.' Therefore, I will boast all the more gladly of my weaknesses, so that the power of Christ may rest upon me."

- Philippians 1:6 "And I am sure of this, that he who began a good work in you will bring it to completion at the day of Jesus Christ."

Overcoming the Fear of Not Being Good Enough

To overcome the fear of not being good enough, it is essential to know your identity in Christ and renew your mind with the truth of God's Word. Things become easier once you recognize that your worth and value come from being a child of God and not what others think about you. You are fearfully and wonderfully made in His image. So, shift your focus from seeking validation from others to seeking approval from God. Know that His opinion of you is the only one that truly matters. Start replacing negative self-talk and thoughts of inadequacy with God's truth. Meditate on scriptures that affirm your worth and remind you of God's love and acceptance.

It can be so comforting to finally understand that you do not have to earn God's love or acceptance. His grace is freely given, and nothing will ever be able to undo that! Embrace His grace, knowing that His love for you is unconditional and not based on your performance. Celebrate your strengths, talents, and passions. Recognize that God has equipped you uniquely for a purpose, and you should celebrate the gifts He has given you and use them to glorify Him. Surround yourself with encouraging people, too. The people around you will always have a major impact on how you see things in life and an influence on the direction your life will take. So, surround yourself with people who affirm your values and remind you of God's love. This is so important.

It may also help tremendously to step out of your comfort zone and take courageous steps toward your dreams and goals. Trust that God will equip and empower you as you step into the plans He has for you. Be kind to yourself and extend grace to yourself just as God extends grace to you. Treat yourself with the same love and compassion you would show to others.

By implementing these strategies and embracing your identity in Christ, you can overcome the fear of not being good enough and walk confidently in the truth that you are chosen, valued, and empowered by God.

15

Fear of Running Out of Time

The fear of not having enough time or running out of time is a common fear that plagues many people and is sometimes referred to as "time anxiety." This fear is a multi-layer fear, referring to not only running out of time in life but also running out of time in everyday life. It can be a fear of constantly being late everywhere you go and the real-world negative effects this can have. So, on the one hand, it can be related to a fear of premature death, and on the other hand, it has so much to do with chronological time.

It is natural to want to arrive at places on time since tardiness can have a negative impact on your success at school or work. But the stress over potential lateness can leave you constantly on edge. You might spend a lot of time checking clocks or planning out the best route to your next destination. This might offer some relief, but at a cost: It distracts you and affects your ability to concentrate on what you are currently doing.

Time anxiety can also affect your mood. If you do show up a few minutes late, you might feel irritated or angry, even when your lateness does not really matter that much. Time anxiety can provoke a desire to rush from one place to the next, often without reason. If you have ever slept longer than intended on a day off, you might have some familiarity with this feeling. When you realize the time, you bolt out of bed, heart pounding, already stressing about lost time and wondering how to catch up.

You may also notice time anxiety showing up in your goals for yourself. Remember your last vacation or weekend? You probably felt excited about the days leading up to that event. Maybe you even made a list of a few tasks to handle at home or enjoyable activities you were looking forward to. Once the vacation began, anxiety hit. You felt the clock ticking off the hours until you had to get back to work or school, and every moment you spent not fulfilling your list of plans felt wasted. And then, once you got back home, you did not even feel satisfied with the things you did manage to do because there was still so much else you could have done. It is the constant feeling that you have missed out on some opportunity because you have run out of time. The real kicker is that this fixation on the passage of time can overwhelm you to the point that you fail to see ways you could have achieved these goals.

One of the key things to understanding time anxiety lies in understanding what causes it. One of those causes is the fear of living a life that has no meaning. This is a life full of dread, which might even include thoughts like "Why am I here?" Or "What is the point of life?" Many times, these kinds of feelings and thoughts are related to a need for control. We want to control how our life goes and how our time is spent. The reality is that we can control some aspects of our lives, but we can never control every single thing that happens in our lives. Knowing that you cannot control certain things like accidents, unforeseen circumstances, or even death can leave you trying to gain greater control in areas where you do have the power, like your daily schedule.

In an online article written for healthline.com in 2020, it is noted that "A fear of showing up late is one way people-pleasing tendencies can manifest. When you want people to like you, you might do everything possible — including being on time — to leave a positive impression. But worrying about what you do with your time can also relate to people-pleasing behaviors. You might reason that failing to use your time in certain ways will disappoint your parents, partner, and other loved ones. When you worry your choices will affect their opinion of you, you might get anxious about making the right choices and fear you will run out of time to correct any mistakes."

The Danger of the Fear of Running Out of Time is that it creates a constant sense of urgency and pressure, leading to chronic stress and anxiety. The fear of running out of time can lead to procrastination and inefficiency as you become overwhelmed by the perceived lack of time and struggle to prioritize your tasks effectively. When you are consumed by this fear, you may miss out on important opportunities or fail to pursue your passions, resulting in regret and unfulfilled potential. You may experience a tendency to "give up" simply because there is no way to accomplish everything that needs to be accomplished in the timeframe you have. It can seem extremely overwhelming to someone who is stuck in this rut.

All of this can strain relationships as you begin to prioritize your tasks over spending quality time with loved ones. Some people also experience anxiety attacks because of the day-to-day stress caused by this type of time anxiety.

Again, this is a particular fear that is not even understandable to a happy-go-lucky person. They tend to think that it is fine to arrive at whatever time they happen to get there. In their minds, there is no real sense of urgency or purpose in arriving on time, and in many cases, they do not even see value in it at all. So, if you happen to be in a relationship with someone who is the polar opposite of you, you may have some homework to do. You may tend to completely disagree with a happy-go-lucky person, emphasizing the importance of being on time and the detrimental effects that come in the real world if you are not. But, at the same time, there is a great value that a happy-go-lucky person can bring to the table, too. Even though it may make more sense to arrive at places on time and avoid negative consequences, there is also a great benefit in ridding your mind of the worry that comes with it.

Here are some Scriptures to Consider:

- Psalm 90:12 "So teach us to number our days that we may get a heart of wisdom."

- Ecclesiastes 3:1 "For everything there is a season, and a time for every matter under heaven."

- Matthew 6:34 "Therefore do not be anxious about tomorrow, for tomorrow will be anxious for itself. Sufficient for the day is its own trouble."

- Psalm 31:15 "My times are in your hand; rescue me from the hand of my enemies and from my persecutors!"

Overcoming the Fear of Running Out of Time

To conquer the fear of running out of time, it is imperative to understand that our times are in God's hands. There are certainly some understandings we can reach regarding healthy time management practices and other practical things, but ultimately, we cannot predict everything that will come our way. It is up to us to make choices that help us balance our life and time. We can learn to clarify our priorities and align them with God's values and goals for us. We can identify what truly matters to us and allocate our time accordingly.

Once you recognize that you have limitations and that it is impossible to do everything, you can set proper realistic expectations for yourself and learn to let go of perfectionism. Learning and implementing effective time management techniques such as creating schedules, setting deadlines, and breaking tasks into manageable steps will go a long way to a brighter future.

It is so important for us to be fully present in each moment and practice mindfulness to combat the tendency to constantly worry about the future or dwell on the past. When we surrender our perception of control over time and trust in God's perfect timing, we begin to recognize that He is the author of time and that His plans for our lives unfold according to His divine schedule. One of the things that our family endeavors to do is consistently incorporate regular rest and Sabbath into our lives. Imagine for a moment what your life would be like if you purposed to dedicate time for rejuvenation, reflection, and personal time with God.

It is so important for us to be fully present in each moment and practice mindfulness to combat the tendency to constantly worry about the future or dwell on the past.

I am not saying that everything is easy, but it is worth it! Learn to identify and eliminate activities or habits that consume your time without adding value or aligning with your priorities. Be intentional about how you spend your time. Seek God's wisdom and guidance in making decisions about how to allocate your time. Pray for discernment and trust that He will lead you in making wise choices. You can fully trust God with your life and your time. One of the things that I personally pray just about every day is, "Lord, I trust you with my life. I trust You with the direction of my life. And I trust you with my time. My times are in Your hands, Lord!" I cannot tell you the amount of relief that comes with a very simple prayer like that. If you are an extreme overthinker and a worrier, a prayer like that can make all the difference in the world.

Finally, I would say that it would be good if you could embrace flexibility and adaptability in your approach to time management. Allow room for unexpected events or changes in plans without allowing them to derail you. You may not always get it right 100% of the time, but you will learn what works and what does not. If you can remain mentally flexible, you will curb your inner anger and frustrations and be able to once again focus on the things that matter the most to you. You are not running out of time; you are trusting God to show you the best use of your time. You can trust God's timing. It will bring supernatural peace to your heart and life.

16

Fear of Disappointing Others

This fear of disappointing others really keeps you running! If you are already dealing with low self-esteem, this fear will certainly remove all remaining dignity you may still have. This fear is rooted in the desire for approval and acceptance from those around you and will stop at nothing to get it. In some ways, the fear of disappointing others is closely tied to the fear of rejection, which we will discuss in a later chapter. The reason this kind of fear keeps you running is that there is no end to the number of people you will try to please. Just think of all the people you already know. Think of the ones you already have in your daily life. Chances are there are quite a few. Once you start down the path of pleasing everyone around you, it will become an endless cycle filled with jumping through hoops. And worse yet, when all the people around you get used to you running around pleasing them, they will only create more ways for you to spin into action — for them! This quickly becomes a difficult habit for them to break, too, and ends up leading to even more pleasing. It is amazing how fast others will take comfort in the ways that you can keep them happy. What a frustrating way to live. It can wear you out! I just got tired thinking about it!

You may not start out thinking this way, but the fear of disappointing others is a very selfish way to live. I can hear you saying, "How in the world can pleasing and satisfying others point to me being selfish?" Here is how. When you are constantly attempting not to disappoint others, the attention is on yourself. It has to do with the "reason" you do not want to disappoint. After all, if you cannot perform in a certain way and meet the needs of those around you, it could end up making you look bad, feel bad, or seem bad — to them. And we cannot have that, can we? For you to remain correct in everyone else's eyes, you must maintain some pretty perfect performance. That is not only difficult to do but impossible to do! You cannot help everybody, satisfy everybody, and please everybody. It is a race you cannot win.

At the same time, I am not saying that you should purposely try not to please, help, and support others. Did you hear that? In fact, this is not so much about your actions to satisfy someone or not, as it is the condition of your heart while you are deciding. There is a balance to this whole thing. I believe you should walk through life with an eye to help others. You should be generous and compassionate. You should hold a servant's heart very close. But I also believe you will remain completely unsatisfied if the fear of pleasing others holds you captive. It is great when others think good of you, but your attention should never be on constantly trying to win their good thoughts. There is a huge difference. It will end up consuming all your mental and emotional energy to stay on everyone's good side. It is simply not worth it. You can easily end up being useless to your closest family and friends by staying in this vicious and impossible cycle.

Sometimes, good solid boundaries need to be set, not only so others will know where you stand on this issue, but so you will also know where you stand. If you constantly second guess yourself while you are in the middle of making a decision to please others, you may need to set some boundaries right now. Again, the goal is not to purposely set out to disappoint others but rather to keep your focus on pleasing God instead. You will ultimately find that it is so much better to walk in this understanding, as God is already on your side and loves you with everlasting love. God loves you and is not disappointed in you. A minister friend of mine has said for years that "God is not mad at you; He is not even in a bad mood!" I love that! Straight to the point.

The Danger of the Fear of Disappointing Others is that you will quite literally waste your life away in service to others but for all the wrong reasons. Although serving others is in line with the true nature of God, doing it out of fear is not. This fear often causes you to constantly seek to please others and sacrifice your own values and desires. This places a heavy emotional burden on you, as you feel responsible for the happiness and approval of everyone around you. If you stay driven by this fear, you may struggle to set healthy boundaries for yourself and may often say yes to others' demands and neglect your own well-being and normal daily responsibilities. The fear of disappointing others often hinders your personal growth in the things of God and causes you to be unfulfilled, too. You may even end up avoiding taking risks altogether or pursuing your own dreams for fear of disappointing those close to you. This is certainly no way to live!

Here are some Scriptures to Consider:

- Galatians 1:10 "For am I now seeking the approval of man, or of God? Or am I trying to please man? If I were still trying to please man, I would not be a servant of Christ."

- Psalm 118:8 "It is better to take refuge in the Lord than to trust in man."

- Romans 12:2 "Do not be conformed to this world, but be transformed by the renewal of your mind, that by testing you may discern what is the will of God, what is good and acceptable and perfect."

- Proverbs 29:25 "The fear of man lays a snare, but whoever trusts in the Lord is safe."

Overcoming the Fear of Disappointing Others

To finally overcome the fear of disappointing others, it is essential to know your identity in Christ and find your security in God rather than in the opinions of people. If you can commit to surround your life with the Word of God, encouraging sermons, good godly relationships, and positive friendships, you will have the strength you need to rid this awful fear from your life.

Keep in mind that the goal here is to come to a place where you understand that God's opinion of you is so far superior to what anyone else may think about you. The truth is that most of the time, they never thought about you at all. It is all a big mind game that you are playing with yourself. It is so much better to rest in knowing that you have God's approval. So, begin to shift your focus from seeking the approval of others to resting in the approval of God. Understand that His opinion of you is what truly matters, and His love and acceptance are unconditional. Begin understanding that when you embrace your true self and live authentically, you will automatically start aligning your actions and decisions with your values and convictions. At some point, you need to recognize that being true to yourself may disappoint some people, but it is essential for your own growth and fulfillment. Nothing lasts forever, and those who may become disappointed in you for some reason will eventually see that you are continuing down a good path and leading a free and happy life. They will get over it.

It is so important to set healthy boundaries to protect your time, energy, and emotional well-being. Learn to say no when necessary and prioritize your own needs without guilt. It is okay to be kind to yourself and extend grace when you make mistakes or fall short of others' expectations. Understand that you are human and that it is impossible to please everyone. It is time for you to focus on your purpose in this life. When you focus on God's true purpose for you, you will see that things will align with that purpose. You will have a clear sense of where you are going in life and it will become easier to prioritize and make decisions that are in line with your calling, even if it means disappointing others.

Sometimes, you must make some tough decisions to rid your life of people and situations that are dragging you down and holding you back. Initially it can be difficult to make those decisions, but in the long run, it is worth it! You know, it is okay to seek relationships where you are accepted and loved for who you are rather than for what you do. Of course, it will work out much better if you can learn to assertively express your needs, desires, and boundaries in a respectful manner. Effective communication can prevent misunderstandings and help build healthier relationships.

---

*When you focus on God's true purpose for you,
you will see that things will align
with that purpose.*

There is such freedom in surrendering control of all this to God. Go ahead and surrender the need to control how others perceive you or react to your decisions. Trust that God will help you and that His plans for your life are ultimately what matters the most. God's strength and guidance will help you navigate challenging situations where you may fear disappointing others. Continue to seek His wisdom and peace as you make decisions that align with His will. You can be rid of this fear forever!

17

Fear of the Unknown

It already sounds like something out of a scary movie, doesn't it? Can't you see it now — some poor soul walking down a dark alley, not knowing what is ahead of him? Then, suddenly, he hears some kind of noise up ahead, some kind of banging or clanging that really sends a chill down your spine. Then, out of nowhere, a cat jumps out and screeches with an ear-piercing sound that you will never forget. All because he just was not sure what to expect. His fate was completely unknown. But it may not be a dark alley that gets the best of you! It might be something as simple as a job change, or a first date, or a big financial decision. No matter what the situation is, the fear of the unknown is a powerful fear that often stems from our natural inclination for security and certainty. We tend to get very comfortable with predictability. Think about it for a second; every day of our lives, we look at our mobile devices to tell us what the weather will be like that day and for the days ahead. When we make investments, we often study the patterns of a particular investment to see its performance in the past, hoping to give us an idea of what it will do in the future. If we purchase a new vehicle, we often read all the consumer reports to make sure we understand all we can about the vehicle to make the best possible decision on whether to purchase it or not. We like patterns, and we really like predictable things. We certainly do not like being caught off guard.

---

*We tend to get very comfortable
with predictability.*

I remember a time when I got completely caught off guard by something. When my oldest daughter was just a few years old, my wife and I were shopping with her at a department store. Somewhere along the way, she decided that she needed to use the restroom. Since my wife was busy looking at some things in the store, I decided to take her to the restroom myself. It seemed like such an easy task, and I had done this with her many times in the past, but this day was a little different. Of course, I had to take her to the men's room as I could not go into the ladies' room. When I arrived at the men's room, I noticed there was already a line that had formed outside of the restroom. So, we waited for a few moments until there was room for us. It was quite crowded in the restroom that day. Once we went inside the restroom, I was good to keep my hand over my young daughter's eyes so that she wouldn't see anything she didn't need to see, and no one else would be nervous about it either. We managed to make our way back to an open stall, went inside, and closed the door behind us. So far, so good! What could possibly go wrong at this point? I helped my daughter go to the restroom as any good father would and then helped her get situated after she finished. Since there was a long line to get into the restroom, I thought that I should probably go ahead and use the restroom myself since we were already there. So, I turned my daughter around so that she could not see anything, and I began to lower my blue jeans so that I could also use the restroom. You need to understand that at this time, wearing boxer shorts with a Hawaiian print on them was very popular, and that's exactly what I had on. For some reason unknown to me, my young daughter turned around quickly to see my Hawaiian print boxers. As soon as she saw those boxer shorts with the Hawaiian print on them, she exclaimed, in a very loud voice, "Daddy, you've got your flower panties on today!" Did I mention that it was an extremely crowded restroom? I cannot begin to tell you the thoughts that ran through my head at that moment. There is no conceivable way to undo what she had just spoken. There was no way to explain it. I didn't see it coming. It was completely unpredictable and unknown. I don't think there is anything that can really prepare you for a thing like that. I was caught completely off guard. Of course, I went ahead and finished what I was there to do, and we began to make our way back out of the restroom. It is hard to explain how many people were looking at me as we left. Who knows what thoughts were having, too? Even after we left the men's room, there were still people in the store who were watching to see who was going to exit. The point is, no one really likes being caught off guard and being put in a compromising or unusual situation. And yet, life is not always predictable. If you doubt that for a second, you can always ask my daughter. True story!

This chapter will explore the nature of the fear of the unknown and its detrimental impact on our lives and provide practical steps to overcome it through faith.

I think most normal people would be okay with the occasional surprise birthday party, but outside of that, we really like to know what is coming before it gets here. We only like surprises to a certain point. It is our human nature to want to know what is just around the corner. Maybe we can chalk that up to a self-preservation instinct that kicks in to protect us, or maybe we are a lot more comfortable having an established plan in place and choosing not to deviate from the plan. In other words, sometimes we like surprises, but we never like surprises that lead us to financial ruin, hurt, pain, or suffering. So, we naturally will do everything we can to avoid anything disrupting our normal world. Of course, the problem here is that the world is constantly changing around us, and we can't possibly predict every outcome that we will face. If we are walking in the fear of the unknown, we will constantly face this fear because we cannot know or understand everything "just around the corner."

Again, this book is not necessarily designed for a whole cross-section of society who is willing to throw caution to the wind and jump off a cliff into an unexplored river below. This information is not designed to speak to explorers of the unknown, test pilots for the aerospace industry, or people who will knowingly scale the outside of a 40-story building just to get an adrenaline rush. No, my friend, this material is written for your benefit. To the one who errs on the side of caution. To the ones who have a need to know what is coming next and are constantly plagued with not knowing.

The Danger of the Fear of the Unknown is that it can significantly negatively affect our lives. Walking in this kind of fear will absolutely prevent you from taking risks or stepping out of your comfort zone. This fear keeps you constantly looking ahead and worrying about life's uncertainties and the future's unpredictability. It keeps you believing that everything is "risky." This leads to anxiety and stress, even chronic stress. It can become very easy to remain trapped in a state of unease and restlessness. It may not seem apparent initially, but this fear often stems from a desire for control. It keeps you clinging to what is familiar and limits your ability to adapt and embrace new experiences. Ultimately, unless this kind of fear is dealt with, you will lead a life trying to control everything and everyone around you to keep things in a very specific order that does not interrupt your life. All of this is a direct response to keeping things very orderly and predictable. But one of the worst things about this kind of fear is that it will consume you to the point that you struggle to trust God's plan and His faithfulness. And this will lead to reduced spiritual growth and a lack of intimacy with God. It is a terrible way to live life!

Here are some Scriptures to Consider:

- Proverbs 3:5-6 "Trust in the Lord with all your heart, and do not lean on your own understanding. In all your ways acknowledge him, and he will make straight your paths."

- Isaiah 41:10 "Fear not, for I am with you; be not dismayed, for I am your God; I will strengthen you, I will help you, I will uphold you with my righteous right hand."

- Joshua 1:9 "Have I not commanded you? Be strong and courageous. Do not be frightened, and do not be dismayed, for the Lord your God is with you wherever you go."

- Psalm 23:4 "Even though I walk through the valley of the shadow of death, I will fear no evil, for you are with me; your rod and your staff, they comfort me."

Overcoming the Fear of the Unknown

To overcome the fear of the unknown, you must surrender the control of your life to God. I do not know of a simpler way to say it, but it is crucial to cultivate deep faith and trust in God, whether you can see what is coming or not. Once you acknowledge that God is leading your life, has a great plan for you, loves you with everlasting love, and wants the very best for you, it will be much easier to surrender your need for control and place your trust in His perfect plan. Anytime you can deepen your relationship with God through prayer, studying His Word, and seeking Him, you will get to know Him and trust Him on a different level. And that will lead to a more secure feeling of His guidance and provision for you. I find that it really helps to reflect on God's faithfulness in my life, too. When you look back on your past experiences and remind yourself of God's faithfulness, and you recall the times that he led you through unknown territories in the past, you will have a greater understanding of how he will provide for all your needs in the future.

I know I have repeated myself many times in this book, but there really is a true strength in meditating on Scripture, which is found in God's word, and participating in worship and fellowship with God. Any time you can engage in activities that deepen your spiritual connection with God, you will come out on top! Instead of worrying about the future or dwelling on uncertainties, focus on the present moment. Practice mindfulness, being fully aware, and embracing what is happening right now. Learn to practice being mindful and present in the current moment. I understand that it takes courage to step out and embrace new experiences, especially when they seem uncertain or unfamiliar, but that is how we develop and grow our trust in God. It is only when we are truly stepping out in faith, completely relying on Him, that we see the greatest results in our lives. Remember, his strength is made perfect in our weakness. Trust that God is with you and will guide you as you step into the unknown.

The Word of God says He will not leave or forsake you. He is not going to leave you high and dry, stranded in the desert, with no means of escape. That is not his nature at all. His ultimate desire is for you to have such trust in Him that you are not afraid to face the unknown because you understand in your heart that he will not let you fall. We have often gotten to the point that we trust more in our schedules and all our ordered events than we do in God. But again, not everything in this world can be predicted, and there will be many times in life when we will face uncertainties. We cannot cower down and move forward at the same time. So, step out! Surround yourself with faith-filled people who can offer support, encouragement, and wisdom as you make choices to walk into the unknown. Share your fears and accept guidance from those who have experienced God's faithfulness. You would be absolutely amazed if you knew how many people around you were facing the very same things that you are facing. Instead of resisting change, view it as an opportunity for growth. Choose to take on the adventure of the unknown, knowing that God is with you every step of the way. Focus on the blessings and goodness of God, recognize His provision in the past, and trust that He will continue to guide you, protect you, and provide for your needs in the future. You already have what it takes to overcome the fear of the unknown, but it all starts with faith in God, trust in his plan, and continued growth and transformation that only comes by spending time with God and reading his Word.

Trust that God is with you and will guide you as you step into the unknown.

18

Fear of Change

This fear was a real challenge for me personally. I am, by nature, a neat and orderly person. I like to have all my ducks in a row and know where the row starts and stops, too. I know it sounds weird, but I like spreadsheets! I like the nice, neat columns and rows — so perfect. I also tend to want things to stay in a certain order once I finally get them there, and that is where the real problem begins. It seems a little funny to me that we even anticipate that things will stay the same when the whole world is constantly changing around us every day, but we do. I think about so many of the people named in the Bible that God greatly used to do extraordinary things, and I also realize that in each situation, those same people had to face massive changes. Can you imagine what it must have been like to be Noah? To hear from God that you were supposed to stop what you were doing and begin the process of building a huge boat in the middle of nowhere. Think of the work and time that took — it was not a weekend project! Not a year-long project, not a ten-year project, not even twenty! It took him many decades. And then to consider that it had never actually rained up to that point makes it even harder. People thought Noah had lost his mind — until it started raining. Yet, Noah was obedient to do what God asked him to do. Talk about a change? But isn't that really the whole point here, to simply be obedient to what God has put in your heart? That is what makes this kind of fear so treacherous. This fear wants to keep you from doing just that. It wants to play upon your natural inclination for comfort and familiarity. I could also say it like this: "The fear of change wants to keep you right where you are!"

It is very difficult, if not impossible, to remain completely comfortable with yourself and obedient to God at the same time! God requires change before advance and move forward. I remember when I was a young boy in school, we would have recess. We would all get so excited and run out to the playground to spend 15 or 20 minutes just playing and having fun. At some point, we would inevitably hang from the monkey bars and try to make it all the way across rung by rung. Of course, we could never actually make any forward progress and move forward until we had let go of the rung that was now behind us. The whole idea is that you had to let go of something in the past and swing forward to grab hold of something that was ahead of you. Yes, it seemed a little scary at first, but then we got the hang of it. No pun intended. Well, the same is true in our normal everyday lives. Sometimes, we just have to let go of something and choose to move on to something new, trusting that it will work out. The fortunate thing in our case is that while we are making the changes, God is still the stable hand that is holding us up from underneath. We have a safety net! And the reason God can require change in us is because He never changes. He becomes the stable rock and the steady hand under us that allows us to change and improve while keeping us safe from the adverse effects of that same change. Another way to say it is that the fear of change keeps us in a constant state of "not trusting" God. As long as you completely trust God, you can make decisions, pursue your dreams, launch out, try new things, and otherwise live an exciting and adventurous life. But the moment you stop trusting God, you draw back. You remain afraid. You don't take risks. Basically, you remain in a permanent position of fear. It's a lot like the loving father who is attempting to teach his young child how to ride a bicycle. The father can run alongside the child, but the child has to actually be on the bike. The father is right there to keep the child upright and moving forward, but the child must pedal the bike. The father is there to provide a safety net so that the child will not crash and injure themselves. The father is available to assist and catch the child if necessary, but it's up to the child to learn to ride the bicycle. Once the child has grasped the concept of riding the bicycle, the fear of this big change suddenly leaves, and the child is free to ride the bicycle for the rest of their life. At that point, the child is usually so free that you can hardly ever find them again, and it takes forever to get them to come home to eat dinner at night. Once they are free, they are completely free! I should know, I have done this exact thing with all seven of our children.

It is very difficult, if not impossible, to remain completely comfortable with yourself and obedient to God at the same time!

Certainly, everyone experiences some level of fear of change from time to time. After all, that's why we have a comfort zone. We like to stay in the comfort zone because it makes us feel comfortable. Science will even tell you that feelings of uncertainty and change feel very similar to feelings of failure and defeat. That may be why so many people would rather avoid any change at all rather than face the uncomfortable feelings of change. It is natural and normal to want to be more educated about something before moving forward. It is understandable to desire more information to make better quality decisions. But when those same feelings become so scary and so serious that it becomes an intense fear of change, it can also paralyze you and cause you to have persistent, unrealistic thoughts that cast doubt and darkness on your future. If this happens each time you face new situations and experiences, it can mean real trouble.

There are many different life experiences where people fear change rather than choosing to make the change, even when making the change is the better decision. A person may choose to stay in a toxic relationship because they fear the alternative of being single or having to date to find someone new. Or when people stay at a dead-end job that makes them miserable or leaves them feeling unsatisfied because they are scared to start something new. Often, the optimal solution would be to move on and try something new, but when you are stuck in a situation and have a fear of change, you cannot see it so clearly. We fear change because our brains are designed to find peace in knowing. When we do not know what will happen, we create scenarios that cause worry and anxiety.

Many times, we may even find it hard to move on when something known comes to an end. Maybe you work on a contract job, and the end of your contract is approaching. You have been working on the same contract for two years straight, but now it is coming to an end. What are you going to do next? What does the future hold? How will you continue to make money? You may have to completely change your job situation, your living situation, your driving situation, and who knows what else. This is where you really learn to trust that God has a plan for your life, and it is up to you to follow that plan. You see, the fear of failure also comes into play to create and prolong this fear of change. If we don't know how something will turn out, we may rather not try at all because we have predetermined that the outcome could be bad, or at least worse than what we had before.

Many contributing factors can add to the fear of change, including current conditions, childhood experiences, your general family view, personal outlooks on life, and even just the way people are programmed. If you have grown up in a household full of cynicism and negativism, you may find it very easy to walk in fear and anxiety when it comes to trying something new. It is not necessarily your fault, but it is something that you are currently facing. The experiences you have grown up with may have created a worldview that promotes thinking that is dangerous or filled with bad outcomes. It would be easy to become jaded in your thoughts if that is what you grew up with. So, instead of making any changes, you find it much easier to stick with what you already know, even if that is negative.

That being said, the fear of change in your mind can be altered, and you can be completely free of it once and for all. It would help you to realize that at one point in your life, everything was unknown. Keep in mind that not everything has to be dealt with in extremes. You may have certain aspects of your life that will require greater change — from finding the right job or choosing your college major to choosing your future spouse. But trying to face all these changes at once is undoubtedly overwhelming. Instead, break things down into smaller pieces. Take things one step at a time. If you want to choose your college major, start by writing down what you like to do and what you are interested in. Then, consider your future job. Next, you can approach things rationally and build up to making the right choices. Choose to take things one step at a time.

The Danger of the Fear of Change is that when you continually cling to the familiar and resist change, you also may unintentionally resist God's plan for your life. This fear ultimately hinders your ability to fully surrender and trust God in His leading, resulting in stagnation and missed opportunities. Fear of change can keep you stuck in your comfort zone, preventing you from pursuing new opportunities altogether. As one minister friend of mine has so accurately stated, "It will keep you in your "fraidy-hole!" Your place of hiding. Resisting changes in your life can lead to regret and constant questioning of what could have been. This fear will also limit your ability to be flexible and adaptable to the inevitable changes that will surround you all your life. It can hinder your capacity to navigate through life's challenges and embrace new seasons.

---

*Resisting changes in your life can
lead to regret and constant questioning
of what could have been.*

Here are some Scriptures to Consider:

- Isaiah 43:19 "Behold, I am doing a new thing; now it springs forth, do you not perceive it? I will make a way in the wilderness and rivers in the desert."

- Psalm 32:8 "I will instruct you and teach you in the way you should go; I will counsel you with my eye upon you."

- Proverbs 16:9 "The heart of man plans his way, but the Lord establishes his steps."

- Romans 8:28 "And we know that for those who love God all things work together for good, for those who are called according to his purpose."

Overcoming the Fear of Change

To overcome the fear of change and step into God's plan, it is crucial to embrace a mindset of trust, surrender, and openness toward God. Remember, God has a pretty amazing track record throughout all of history. He has always operated in a manner that deserves your unwavering trust. Each of us should take comfort in knowing that he has a divine purpose and a plan for our lives, even if that means making some changes along the way. Since we can place complete confidence in the fact that He will not change and will always support what he has already shown us in the Word of God, we can approach Him boldly and receive his help right when we need it. The Bible clearly shows that God has already given us everything pertaining to life and godliness. We can also clearly see that those things come through the knowledge of Jesus Christ. The real question is whether we will take the time to get to know Jesus better to unlock the very things that we desperately need in our lives. Once we take the steps to approach God through prayer, receive his wisdom, and cultivate the Word of God in our hearts by having a listening ear, we will see that He is ready to lead and direct our steps every day. God's ways are higher than our ways, and he can see the end from the beginning. God has a unique vantage point in our lives that puts Him in a position to accurately guide us every step of the way. We just have to trust Him. When you think about it, change does not have to be fearful at all. Change can be a wonderful opportunity for learning, growth, and new experiences. There are many positive things that can come through change and transformation in our lives.

There is no hope of ever controlling every aspect of our lives and predicting everything that will come our way. This is why it is best for us to surrender all our control to God, knowing He will accomplish what is best for us. We need to allow Him to guide and shape our path as we are walking on it. One of the most powerful things you could ever do is replace your fear-based thinking with the truths found in God's Word. This only comes by meditating on the scriptures that remind you of God's faithfulness, his everlasting love, and his ability to work things together for your good.

If our faith and trust are truly in God, we should have no problem taking courageous steps forward, even if they involve uncertainty or uncomfortable choices. When we step out in faith to walk in obedience to what God has put in our hearts, then God provides the strength and the resources we need as we walk into new seasons and new opportunities. As a safeguard, it is always a good idea to seek wise counsel and remain accountable to others as we navigate different transition periods. Change can seem very awkward at times, but always leads to advanced steps of progress. Wise counsel from other godly people will help us maintain a steady course and ensure that we are making decisions that are in line with God's word.

I can't even begin to tell you how important it is to develop a habit of gratitude, focusing on God's blessings and goodness during changing times. It will always be appropriate to have a heart of gratitude for his guidance and his provision throughout every season of our lives. We must embrace the change we come across on life's journey and understand that real growth and transformation often come through seasons of change. Change is good! Change can seem difficult at times. But knowing that God's faithful and steady hand is holding us up every step of the way should give us the courage we need to step out and embrace what the future holds for us, no matter what.

19

Fear that Things
Will Never Change

There are a couple of things that become very apparent when you start talking about these kinds of fears. The first thing you realize is that fear is not from God. The Bible makes it very clear that God has not given us the spirit of fear. It comes from our enemy, the devil. God has a wonderful plan for each of our lives, and he desires so greatly to fulfill us in different ways. He knows exactly what each person needs and when they need it. On the other hand, the devil is out to do anything he can to pull us down and destroy God's plan for our lives so that we cannot fulfill it. The primary way that our enemy operates against us is through deception in our own minds, and that is why fear is such a big deal. So, when we start talking about the fear that things will never change, we need to also understand that in the last chapter, we just dealt with the exact opposite of this: the fear of change. Can you see how the devil operates? If he cannot get you one way, he will just try the opposite way! If he cannot get you coming, he will try to get you going! That is exactly what this fear is all about. It is just a second attempt to throw you off track if the first one does not work. And the crazy thing is that the devil never really comes up with any different plan. He just continues to attack you in the same old ways he always has. Keep in mind that his entire focus is to steal from you, kill you if he can, and destroy your life. If he was not earnestly seeking these things, he would not be a very good devil, would he?

The fear that things will never change can keep you from breakthroughs in your life. In much the same way that the fear of change tries to keep you stagnant and still, this fear tries to push you ahead before the right time. This fear plays against patience. It constantly reminds you that things are taking way too long and that you must go ahead and make a move now. Even if you do not have good information or know what you are doing, this fear will prompt you to move forward anyway.

I do not know if you have ever gotten your car stuck in the mud, but it is an awful feeling. It is a helpless feeling. It seems like no matter what you do, it is completely useless to fight against the elements at work against you. I remember a time before I was married when my wife and I were still dating, and I was driving her back home after dinner. I admit it: I got turned around on a back road and lost track of where I was. To get back on the main road I took a shortcut through unfamiliar territory, and before I knew it, my car was completely stuck in deep mud. It was embarrassing and humiliating. Worse yet, I seriously could not get the car out of the mud. I tried doing all the things you are supposed to do, to no avail. My tires were spinning freely, and I was going nowhere fast. And let me also mention that at this point, I was also drenched in mud from my head to my shoes. Eventually, after many attempts, we were able to get the car free and continue to the house. But I will never forget the awful feeling that comes with being stuck. The feeling that you cannot move. Mud is not the only thing that you can be stuck in, though, jobs work just as well! I also know what it feels like to be stuck in a job situation without seeing a way out. When everything in your mind is screaming to you that there is no way out! It is a horrible feeling. Being stuck is drudgery, overwhelming, and mentally anguishing. I think it is safe to say that no one likes to be stuck.

There is, however, a vast difference between being stuck in something and eventually finding your way out and being stuck in something, having no hope that things will ever change. That is where the real problem comes in: when you are stuck and have no hope of freeing yourself. That is where the real fear begins. It is a feeling of hopelessness that leads to anxiety. All the anxiety then prompts you to begin overthinking the situation. Then, it is easy to take the next step of logically creating unrealistic scenarios that lead to nowhere. Can you see how this is one giant, vicious cycle the devil plays in your mind, hoping you will buy the deception and play along? Because if he can get you to play along, he can completely divert your path from accomplishing what God has put in your heart. It is a trick!

The Danger of the Fear that Things Will Never Change is that you remain wrapped up mentally. When your mind is so occupied with the thoughts of dread and hopelessness that come from being stuck in something, you lose all motivation and settle for something less than God's best in your life. All these terrible thoughts end up undermining your faith and trust in God's ability to help you and bring transformation and breakthrough in your life. This kind of fear can completely erode your confidence in God's promises and ultimately lead to doubting God's plan altogether. How terrible!

One of the other things that happens when you feel like you are stuck is that it also becomes very easy to notice everyone else flying by you at light speed. That is when you notice how everyone around you is succeeding at something, and you are still standing there, stuck in the mud of life. Someone else got the job that you were hoping for. You were hoping to go ahead and get married and start a family, and yet that very thing is happening for everyone around you but not you. It was supposed to be you who got accepted into that college, but it wasn't, it was your close friend. See, when you continue to hold onto the belief that things will never change, you also get blinded to the opportunities and blessings God is bringing your way right now. You can easily begin to overlook or completely dismiss the potential you have and the positive transformation that God is attempting to bring into your life. Basically, you end up accepting a limited vision and a reduced potential. Ouch! This kind of fear can restrict you from stepping out in faith, pursuing the dreams that God has put in your heart, and grabbing hold of your God-given potential. It keeps you trapped in a cycle of doubt and complacency.

You can easily begin to overlook or completely dismiss the potential you have and the positive transformation that God is attempting to bring into your life.

Here are some Scriptures to Consider:

- Isaiah 43:18-19 "Remember not the former things, nor consider the things of old. Behold, I am doing a new thing; now it springs forth, do you not perceive it? I will make a way in the wilderness and rivers in the desert."

- Ecclesiastes 3:1 "For everything there is a season, and a time for every matter under heaven."

- Jeremiah 29:11 "For I know the plans I have for you, declares the Lord, plans for welfare and not for evil, to give you a future and a hope."

- Romans 8:28 "And we know that for those who love God all things work together for good, for those who are called according to his purpose."

Overcoming the Fear that Things Will Never Change

To overcome the fear that things will never change, spend some time meditating on and declaring God's promises over your life. Remind yourself of His faithfulness throughout history and in your personal journey. Trust that He is true to His Word. This is the best time to renew your mind using the Word of God. Guard your mind against negative and limiting thoughts. Replace thoughts of despair and doubt with truths from God's Word. Fill your mind with hope, faith, and trust in God's faithfulness. Draw near to God through prayer, worship, and intimate fellowship with Him, and allow His presence to bring peace, strength, and reassurance during seasons of waiting. We all face times in our lives when we wish things would move faster. There are a lot of things that we think we need in this life: houses, cars, and food. But the Bible declares that there is one thing that we need: patience. The Bible says in Hebrews 10:36 (KJV) "For ye have need of patience, that, after ye have done the will of God, ye might receive the promise." That is not necessarily fun to hear, but it is true. So, develop patience and perseverance as you wait on God's timing. Keep pressing forward in obedience and faith, even when things seem stagnant. Trust that God is at work, even in the unseen.

Learn to surrender your timeline and expectations to God. Trust that He has a perfect plan for your life and that His timing is always purposeful and strategic. Consider God's perspective on your circumstances. Ask Him to help you see beyond the present moment and align your perspective with His eternal purposes. Keep a heart of gratitude for the present moment and the blessings that surround you. Try to recognize and appreciate the goodness of God, even amid waiting.

I think it is so important to continually seek God's guidance and walk in obedience to His leading. Trust that as you align your life with His will, He will bring about the necessary changes in His perfect timing. One of the best ways to do this is to make sure you recognize and celebrate the small victories and progress along the way. Acknowledge the ways in which God is already working in your life, and trust that He will continue to bring about continuous positive change. By trusting in God's timing, releasing the fear that things will never change, and actively walking in faith, you can experience the fullness of God's promises and embrace the transformative work He desires to do in your life.

20

Fear of Public Speaking

Most scientific studies agree that the fear of public speaking affects roughly half of the population. Many people tend to feel nervous at the very thought of public speaking, while others experience full-on panic and fear. So why are people so afraid of speaking publicly? Well, the fear of public speaking is not so much related to what is being spoken but rather how the person feels, thinks, or acts when faced with public speaking. There are numerous reasons why people become afraid when having to speak in public. One of the main factors involves a person's beliefs about themselves as speakers. The fear sometimes arises when people overestimate the stakes of communicating their ideas in front of others. When you truly believe negative views of yourself as a public speaker and begin to think that you are not good in front of crowds or you are boring, this can raise your anxiety level and enhance your fears.

Fear of public speaking can prevent you from taking risks and sharing your ideas. It can keep you from speaking about your work and presenting solutions to problems that may affect others. As a result, it can also affect how much you grow personally and professionally and how much impact you can have on those around you. Fear teaches you to protect yourself from risky situations, and the fear of public speaking could easily be perceived as a risky situation. After all, who would want to stand in front of a crowd and embarrass themselves?

There can also be a difference between public performance and public communication. A performance role is usually tied to the belief that there is a special skill needed, and the audience sits as judges who are evaluating how skilled you are. Communication, on the other hand, may mean that the entire focus is on expressing your ideas and presenting information with the objective of getting through to your audience in the same way you would communicate during everyday conversations. Both can be challenging.

Maybe you were one of those people who, by nature, tend to be more anxious or who do not think they are good at public speaking due to certain situations such as a lack of experience or level of education. Keep in mind that, as with anything else, experience builds confidence, and when you don't have many stage hours under your belt, you are more likely to experience fear of public speaking. Even something as simple as a difference in status could drastically affect how you feel before you get up and speak. If you are about to speak in front of people of higher status, higher positions, or groups of accomplished professionals, you may feel a higher dose of fear running through your body.

Consider Moses for a moment. In the Old Testament, God appeared to Moses in the form of a burning bush and asked him to go to Egypt to tell Pharaoh to set his people free. Moses then turned around and asked the Lord to pardon him because he was not eloquent in speech but was slow in speech and tongue. Basically, he was telling God that he was no good at speaking and, therefore, could not carry out this task. In chapter 4 of Exodus, Moses asked the Lord to send someone else instead of him. What a request! Can you imagine standing toe to toe with God Almighty in the middle of the desert and giving him all your excuses? All the reasons why you are not capable of doing what he asked you to do. Moses kept coming up with a long string of excuses about how he was not skilled enough to speak publicly, but God answered each of his questions, one by one. Living proof that God will always find a way to help you in whatever situation you are in. Even when our situation seems very difficult, or maybe even impossible, God can still make a way for us!

Even when our situation seems very difficult,
or maybe even impossible,
God can still make a way for us!

The Danger of the Fear of Public Speaking is that avoiding it can chip away at your self-confidence and self-esteem. It can reinforce a negative self-perception and perpetuate the belief that you are not capable of speaking in public. That would be a real shame since you have so much to offer. This fear can cause you to stumble over your words, forget important points, or fail to connect with your audience. It undermines your ability to convey your message with clarity and conviction. It would be senseless to allow something like this to prevent you from seizing opportunities to share your thoughts, ideas, and experiences with others. More than likely, you honestly want to have a positive influence on others, and you cannot allow this fear to keep you from that. The fear of public speaking creates ongoing limitations in your life and keeps you from utilizing the skills and the potential that you have inside.

Here are some Scriptures to Consider:

- Exodus 4:10-12 "But Moses said to the Lord, 'Oh, my Lord, I am not eloquent, either in the past or since you have spoken to your servant, but I am slow of speech and of tongue.' Then the Lord said to him, 'Who has made man's mouth? Who makes him mute, deaf, or seeing, or blind? Is it not I, the Lord? Now therefore go, and I will be with your mouth and teach you what you shall speak.'"

- Proverbs 16:23-24 "The heart of the wise makes his speech judicious and adds persuasiveness to his lips. Gracious words are like a honeycomb, sweetness to the soul and health to the body."

- 1 Corinthians 2:4 "And my speech and my message were not in plausible words of wisdom, but in demonstration of the Spirit and of power."

- Philippians 4:13 "I can do all things through him who strengthens me."

Overcoming the Fear of Public Speaking

Fortunately for all of us, there is a solution to the fear of public speaking. It is called human generosity! The key to calming yourself down and taking your finger off the panic button is to turn the focus away from ourselves. Away from whether we will mess up or whether the audience will like us — and toward helping the audience.

Studies have shown that kindness and generosity to others have been shown to activate positive nerves in our bodies, which has the power to calm us and reduce our fight-or-flight response. When we are kind to others, we feel calmer and less stressed. The same principle applies to public speaking. When we approach speaking with a spirit of generosity, we counteract the sensation of being under attack and start to feel less nervous. I'm not trying to say that this is super easy, but I am saying that it will help.

So, the next time you are studying to speak, preparing a presentation, or practicing for a performance, think about your audience first. Start with the audience. Before diving into the information, ask yourself: Who will be in the room? Why are they there? What do they need? Identify the audience's needs and prepare a message that speaks directly to those needs.

You will generally be the most nervous right before you speak. This is the moment where your brain is telling you, "Everyone is judging me. What if I fail?" And it is exactly at this moment that you can refocus your brain. Remind yourself that you are here to help your audience. Tell yourself, "Brain, this presentation is not about me. It is about helping my audience." Over time, your brain will begin to get it, and you will become less nervous. One of the biggest mistakes we make is speaking to people as a group. We scan the room — trying to look at everyone at once — and end up connecting with nobody. Keep in mind that each person in the room is listening to you as an individual. The best way to connect to your audience is by speaking to them as individuals.

By focusing on one person at a time, you make each person in the room feel like you are just talking to them.

Of course, it will always be a good idea to have proper preparation before you speak, an outline of what you are going to say, and some good old-fashioned practice in delivering your lines. If you can just take the time to familiarize yourself with the material you are going to present, it will make you feel much more comfortable and confident. Build your confidence by becoming well-versed in your subject matter. The more knowledgeable you are, the more secure you will feel about sharing your thoughts with others.

If it helps you, use visual aids, such as slides or props, to enhance your presentation and provide additional support. I have done this myself for many years. I enjoy using some kind of prop when I speak publicly. I feel like, most of the time, it can really add an element of understanding to what I'm saying. Visual aids can help guide your speech and alleviate some of the pressure of speaking alone. Please understand that no speaker is perfect. Embrace your imperfections and view them as part of your unique style. Authenticity and vulnerability can often resonate with an audience on a deeper level. Our pastor does this all the time when he speaks. Often, he will tell a funny story about something that has happened recently or even make fun of himself and become very vulnerable. This has a unique way of breaking down walls with people and allowing them to open up their heart and freely receive what is being said. It works! So, shift your focus away from your own fears and onto the value of your message and the needs of your audience. Embrace a mindset of service and purpose, seeking to deliver meaningful content that benefits those listening.

Attempt to purposely focus on the positive instead of the negative. Imagine yourself speaking confidently and effectively. Imagine what it would be like to have a solid, positive outcome where your audience was engaged. This will help you rewire your mind for success. Place your trust completely in God, knowing that He equips and empowers you for the tasks He calls you to. Learn to rely on His strength, wisdom, and guidance as you step out of your comfort zone and speak before others.

Attempt to purposely focus on the positive instead of the negative.

21

Fear of Not Knowing What to Say

I don't know exactly when it happened, but we have been programmed to feel very uncomfortable during times of silence. Even though silence can be hugely beneficial to us, we shy away from it and avoid it as often as we can. We have even gotten to the point that we feel a time of silence is an awkward time. There are many places throughout the Bible where it says "Selah." That word means to pause and think about something calmly. When was the last time you took an extra-long moment to sit quietly and think about something? I mean to really take some time and think something through. I remember growing up as a young boy in Florida, how fun it was just to hammer a nail into a board. How fun it was just to tie a rope around a tree and climb it. Or just to ride my bicycle with the wind blowing in my face. I remember many times that I nailed two boards together and pretended that it was an airplane. I had endless hours of fun, just playing out in the yard with two boards. Times were much simpler I guess. Later in life, I remember the first time I saw someone with a calculator. I was amazed that something so small could do so much. Of course, that seems incredibly simple by today's standards. Simple and silence seem to go together. Have you ever had a close friend that you could spend time with and just sit there and enjoy each other's company without having to talk a lot? Some of the most important things in life seem to happen during times of simplicity and silence. The Bible even says to, "Be still and know that I am God."

Some of the most important things in life seem to happen during times of simplicity and silence.

So, how did things get so complicated? How did things get so busy? It sure seems like the more gadgets that are introduced along the way, the more complicated life gets. I don't know how old you are, but I am in my mid-50s at the time of this writing. I remember what life was like before mobile phones, the Internet, artificial intelligence, notifications, texting, and all the popular social media sites. I remember a time when there was nothing that buzzed, dinged, popped, rang, or whistled. It was a pretty quiet time. I am certainly not against any of those things, but they do tend to be large distractions at times. So why would I even bring all this up? Why would I talk about silence and simplicity in the middle of a chapter that is supposed to be about the fear of not knowing what to say? Because we have all become so used to having every possible second of every possible day filled with something that gets our attention. We have grown so accustomed to having every spare moment filled with something that makes noise, produces music, notifies us, or gets our attention in some way that we have completely lost the art of having times when nothing is happening. I think that is kind of sad.

Part of the reason that there is a fear of not knowing what to say is that we become paralyzed and feel inadequate or anxious when every moment is not filled with something to say. We feel like there needs to be a continuous stream of conversation or noise of some kind all the time. We can feel the pressure of always having to say something or always having an answer to something when sometimes it might be best not to say anything at all. I understand that there are times when you will need to say something or present some type of information, and we will get to that in a moment. But, at this moment, I would like you to be relieved of the pressure of constantly having to perform. To constantly fill every moment with something that makes noise. Learn to be at peace and be relaxed in the moment. Once you learn to do this, you will find that it is during those relaxing, peaceful, and silent times that you will know what to say when it is your turn. God is always very faithful to provide the words for you to say if you will only take the time to go to him and listen. The funny thing about listening is that it is very difficult to listen and talk at the same time. We need to learn the fine art of going to God and listening to what he has to say instead of telling him all of the things that are on our minds.

Now, when it is your turn to present information or have something to say, I understand that there can also be a paralyzing pressure that makes you feel inadequate and anxious. Most of the time, this is due exclusively to uncertainty. As we have discussed in previous chapters, we do not like uncertainty in our lives. We do not like it when we stand before people, not knowing exactly what to say or what the next steps are. I am talking about those wonderful times when someone comes to you with an impromptu request to get up and "say a few words." Maybe someone will ask you to describe something or make a short speech about something at a wedding or other gathering of people. Maybe it is a time at a church gathering or a small group when someone asks you to stand up and start the service by praying. Oh, the terror that fills your heart when you are asked to do something at the last second, and you are not prepared at all. Your heart starts to pound, you start to sweat, your tongue swells up in your mouth, and your mind goes completely blank. The biggest problem is that the situation was unexpected and sudden; it seems there is no escaping it. You have now been put in a situation where all the attention is put on you, and you do not know what to do or say. I get it. It can be terrifying. Okay, that is the bad news, but we are going to get to the good news shortly. First, let's talk about the dangers of this kind of fear.

The Danger of the Fear of Not Knowing What to Say is that it produces ineffective communication as a result of hesitation, awkwardness, and difficulty in expressing yourself. It can completely hinder you from conveying your ideas and feelings clearly. If you remain in a constant state of this fear, it will undermine your self-confidence and your self-esteem. It will absolutely perpetuate an overall negative self-perception and reinforce the belief that you are incapable of engaging in meaningful conversations. If you cannot engage in good conversation, then you will also miss out on establishing connections with others. This can easily hinder you from developing authentic relationships with other people. It is a perpetual negative cycle. This can cause you to struggle with asserting yourself and expressing your thoughts, needs, and opinions. All this only leads to feelings of frustration and dissatisfaction. On top of everything else, it can be extremely embarrassing.

Here are some Scriptures to Consider:

- Proverbs 15:23 "To make an apt answer is a joy to a man, and a word in season, how good it is!"

- Luke 12:12 "For the Holy Spirit will teach you in that very hour what you ought to say."

- Proverbs 18:4 "The words of a man's mouth are deep waters; the fountain of wisdom is a bubbling brook."

- Colossians 4:6 "Let your speech always be gracious, seasoned with salt, so that you may know how you ought to answer each person."

Overcoming the Fear of Not Knowing What to Say

I think one of the keys to overcoming this fear is to focus on actively listening to the other person instead of being solely concerned about what you will say next. If you truly listen, you can gain valuable insights and be able to respond thoughtfully. If you are unsure about a specific topic or situation, do not hesitate to ask questions. It is okay to be curious and willing to learn while also keeping the conversation flowing. I think it is a good idea to continually enhance your knowledge and broaden your perspectives on a variety of topics through reading, research, and continuing education. The more you learn, the more equipped you will be to have engaging conversations.

Again, it is also so important to show empathy by seeking to understand the other person's point of view, emotions, and experiences. This will give you the greatest chance to respond with a true, compassionate heart and genuine interest. Take a moment to find some common ground or shared interest with the other person in the conversation. This will help you establish a connection and create a positive foundation for the rest of the conversation. Many times, the other person will say something that sparks you to say something. Sometimes, all it takes is one small spark to initiate a lengthy conversation. I think you'll be pleasantly surprised how your thoughts will begin to flow if you just pay attention. It does not have to be difficult, but sometimes we make it difficult. Change the way you think about it. As we already discussed, it is okay to be quiet or take a moment of silence before you begin speaking. Learn to express your thoughts and feelings authentically and avoid pretending to know everything about every situation. Sometimes, we need to be vulnerable in our interactions. People put up so many besides these days that you might be the first bright spot in someone's day or life by just being genuine.

Attempt to stay present in the conversation and practice being mindful of the overall conversation. Allow the Holy Spirit to guide you in moments of uncertainty, and trust that the Holy Spirit will provide you with wisdom, insight, and the right words to say in each situation. Be aware of your thoughts and emotions, and intentionally focus on the moment at hand instead of worrying about what to say next. And cut yourself some slack and give yourself some grace. I understand that every future conversation will not go perfectly. Mistakes do happen, and it is an opportunity to grow and learn. **Let go of**

perfectionism and embrace the journey of becoming a better communicator. Just putting these few things into practice will completely revolutionize your confidence level and your ability to communicate with others.

22

Fear of Horrifying Death and Diseases

If you have never experienced the fear of horrifying death and disease, you should take a moment right now and count your many blessings! If you have experienced these things, brace yourself, this chapter will probably hit hard.

There is nothing in the world quite like the sensation that your time is up, you have come to the end, there is no road ahead, there is no future for you, and you are about to leave your family and loved ones behind to an uncertain future. If you know, you know! If you do not, you are blessed!

Of all the different kinds of fears that we have discussed, this one has to be among the worst. This one has a finality attached to it like none of the others. To experience this kind of fear is to know that everything has come to an end and there is no hope of a future. Not only is there a huge uncertainty attached to this fear, but it can also hit you from almost any direction at any time. Let's be honest for just a moment and have a straightforward conversation. If you are the kind of person who has dealt with this kind of fear, these next paragraphs will feel very common to you. This fear presents you with the idea that you are about to die. This fear makes sure that you are aware that your death will not be quick, but it will be horrible. This fear specifically focuses on the suffering that will occur in your mind and in your body before you die. It puts the emphasis on the fact that death is certain, and it is coming for you anytime now. After all, you could be in a horrible automobile accident the next time you drive. That short airplane ride you are about to take could end in a terrifying crash that takes the life of everyone on board. That vacation float trip down the popular river of your dreams could easily end in your drowning. The next check-up you receive from the doctor will be the time that he thumps you on the chest and tells you that you only have a short period of time to live, and it will be a horrifying short time full of suffering and pain.

I think I already adequately explained this in earlier chapters, but these kinds of thoughts are very real to those who are facing this kind of fear. They probably will not mean much at all to those "happy-go-lucky" people who never really seem to have any trouble with this sort of thing. Some people would read what I have just written and laugh, not understanding that these thoughts and feelings are quite real to others. They could even be tempted to not have compassion on those who face these kinds of things. Make no mistake about it: fear is terrible, and fear is a tormenting thing. It torments your mind.

The fear of horrible death and diseases will keep you awake at night while your family sleeps peacefully. They can be getting a good night's rest, but you cannot go to sleep because of the thoughts that are going through your mind, clicking away like the shutter on a camera. Over and over, the thoughts come to you of dying in your sleep and leaving your family behind. Thoughts of cancer. Thoughts of heart disease and heart attacks. Thoughts of blood clots and a myriad of other physical problems that are specifically designed to take you out and cause the most suffering possible in the process. I am not kidding here! These things are very, very real to those who experience them. I was one of those people! I know what it is like to stay up all night long, night after night, truly believing in my heart that I was going to die. Constantly checking to make sure that our life insurance policies were up to date so that at least my family would have something to help them financially after I died. Constantly writing things down to make sure that my remaining family would have the pertinent information at their fingertips upon my demise. It can sound so silly, but it is no laughing matter. I remember so many times after my family would go to sleep that I would go out into the living room and just cry. I would cry because I was thinking about having to leave them. I would cry because I knew I would not be around to help them. I would cry because I would not be there to walk my daughters down the aisle when they got married. I would cry because I wouldn't get to show my sons how to ride a bicycle or shoot a basketball. This is an extreme fear!

The fear of horrible death and diseases is most often based on the experiences that you have seen in others. It is a false translation of something you have seen that has been related in your mind to your own life. There is nothing that is connected in any way to someone else, yet in your mind, you have applied the same criteria to your own physical body. In other words, if I watched some terrible things happen to someone else, more than likely, it is going to happen to me, too. If I knew someone from high school who had this terrible disease, I would most likely get the same treatment. It is a constant comparison game. It will not let your mind rest until you are free from it. This fear will grip you with anxiety, worry, and a sense of powerlessness, and it will try to hold on tight. I know what it is like to be bound by it, and I know what it is like to be free from it. Trust me, freedom is better!

The Danger of the Fear of Diseases and Horrifying Death is that it keeps your mind bound. It keeps you constantly considering your own death. It keeps death as the foremost thought in your mind and the talk of death on the tip of your tongue. It completely impairs the quality of your life and consumes you. It diminishes everything about your life. It keeps you from enjoying the life that you have by tying you up with a continual stream of "what if" situations. Forget about engaging in meaningful relationships or activities; you will not even be able to keep your mind on the people around you. It is debilitating and has extremely negative consequences attached to it. This fear most often manifests itself as heightened anxiety and worry about your health and the potential for horrific death. It only leads to chronic stress, sleep anxiety, and a continual string of physical ailments. It is like a horrible, self-fulfilling prophecy. The more your mind thinks about it, the more you concentrate on it, the higher likelihood you will have of experiencing actual physical problems in your body. The stress, fear, anxiety, and overthinking process alone are enough to cause physical problems in your body. Because this fear utilizes worry so effectively, it may also keep you from ever visiting the doctor for fear of what the doctor will find. Even if there is nothing to find, the fear alone will keep you away from the doctor. This process may prevent you from seeking necessary medical attention or a timely intervention. If you delay medical care for your physical body, you could have health conditions that result in unfavorable outcomes, all because you were walking in fear and did not want to hear what the doctor had to say.

It completely impairs the quality of your life and consumes you.

Constant fear can erode faith and hope, causing you to question God's goodness and provision in the face of illness and mortality.

Here are some Scriptures to Consider:

- Psalm 23:4 "Even though I walk through the valley of the shadow of death, I will fear no evil, for you are with me; your rod and your staff, they comfort me."

- Isaiah 41:10 "Fear not, for I am with you; be not dismayed, for I am your God; I will strengthen you, I will help you, I will uphold you with my righteous right hand."

- 2 Timothy 1:7 "For God gave us a spirit not of fear but of power and love and self-control."

- Romans 8:38-39 "For I am sure that neither death nor life, nor angels nor rulers, nor things present nor things to come, nor powers, nor height nor depth, nor anything else in all creation, will be able to separate us from the love of God in Christ Jesus our Lord."

Overcoming the Fear of Diseases and Horrifying Death

To overcome the fear of diseases and horrifying death, consider cultivating a trusting relationship with God. It is up to you to strengthen your relationship with God through prayer, meditation, and studying His Word. Trust in His character, love, and faithfulness, knowing that He is with you in every circumstance. Learn to practice mindfulness and focus on the present moment rather than dwelling on future uncertainties. Embrace gratitude for each day and find joy and happiness in the blessings and experiences of life. God made you, and He knows how to care for you!

Educate yourself and seek accurate information about diseases and health conditions from reliable sources. Understanding the facts can alleviate irrational fears and help you to make informed decisions about your health. Take proactive steps to maintain your physical and mental well-being. Adopt a healthy lifestyle, engage in regular exercise, eat a balanced diet, and prioritize self-care. Taking care of your health can provide a sense of control and empowerment. Surround yourself with a supportive community of friends, family, or a faith-based group that can provide encouragement, prayer, and emotional support during challenging times. Share your concerns and fears with trusted people who can walk alongside you.

Practice self-compassion! Be kind and compassionate to yourself, recognizing that fear and anxiety are normal human experiences. Allow yourself to feel and process emotions while extending grace to yourself. Seek professional help if you need to.

Ground your faith in the hope found in Jesus Christ. Meditate .on the promises of God's presence, provision, and eternal life. Let your faith be a source of strength and comfort in times of uncertainty. Serve and impact others. Shift your focus from your own fears to serving and making a positive impact on others. Engage in acts of kindness, support those in need, and contribute to your community. Serving others can bring purpose and fulfillment.

Embrace the gift of life and live each day to the fullest. Pursue your passions, build relationships, and find joy in simple pleasures. Fix your gaze on the eternal perspective. There is a wonderful older hymn called "Turn your eyes upon Jesus."

The song says:

Turn your eyes upon Jesus

Look full in his wonderful face

And the things of earth will grow strangely dim

In the light of his glory and grace

His word shall not fail you he promised

Believe him and all will be well

Then go to a world that is dying

His perfect salvation to tell

Remember that as believers, our hope extends beyond this earthly life. The promise of eternal life with God brings comfort and assurance.

By implementing these strategies and anchoring yourself in faith, hope, and the love of God, you can overcome the fear of diseases and horrifying death.

Whew! That was a difficult chapter to write.

23

Fear of Not Being Prepared

We have probably all heard of the "preppers." Who knows, you might be one! That amazing section of society seems to be ready for anything. They are standing at the ready with tents and boxes of matches, canned food, animal traps, bomb shelters, generators, and the ability to start a campfire with only two sticks. These are the people who are ready for anything. Maybe they are preparing for the end of the world. Maybe they are preparing for the coming zombie apocalypse. Maybe they just want to get away for the weekend. Maybe I'm talking about you! Are you a "prepper?" Are you prepared for anything? Probably not. In either case, it is most likely better to be prepared than unprepared.

I guess I would consider myself somewhat of a prepared person. I make sure that the spare tire in my car is full of air in case I have a flat tire. I make sure that my gas tank is not running on fumes so that I'm not left stranded on the side of the road. I usually make sure I have at least $20 in my wallet just in case I need a little cash for some emergency. I usually leave the house a few minutes sooner than I need to just in case there is bad traffic. After all, I want to be prepared and still get to my destination on time. I would say I am prepared! You should see what I go through when my wife and I travel. I tend to prepare for almost any situation we could encounter. I make sure to have a light jacket in case it is cold, a rain jacket in case there is a storm, an extra pair of shoes in case we walk a lot, and even extra underwear just in case . . . well. Did you notice how many times in the last paragraph I used the word "extra" and the phrase "just in case?" That's right, I always have extra things just in case things don't go well. But there is a vast difference between being somewhat prepared for the coming situation and the fear of constantly worrying that you are unprepared. I used to walk in fear, but now I have dropped the fear, and I am just prepared. I like this a lot better! Of course, there is still that section of society that is completely satisfied with remaining unprepared. The adventurers who would much rather start driving in any direction and just figure it out as they go. They are the ones who book those cheaper last-minute flights to unknown destinations just for the fun of it. Well, God bless you; that is just not me!

As with many of the fears we are discussing, this particular fear also finds its roots in feelings of inadequacy and uncertainty. No one likes the feeling you have when you are behind and trying to catch up. No one likes to be left behind, but this fear goes a step further and causes you to be terrified of making mistakes. It is an obsessive fear that points out your imperfections so that you will avoid any situation where you feel you will not succeed. It brings with it the sensation of free, falling, and not being able to grasp anything to hold onto. It is like having the rug pulled out from under you. This fear will keep you in a constant position of not feeling ready. You may tend to make sure you turn off the iron or the stove before you leave the house, and that would be normal. But when you must check those same things five to ten times before you walk out the door, you are walking in fear. When you constantly feel your pockets to make sure you have your keys, or enough money in your pocket, or your purse, or your wallet. This fear simply takes things too far. You might even say this fear exaggerates each situation and blows it completely out of proportion.

It can even be closely related to the fear of not knowing what to say. Imagine the nightmare of standing on a stage, speechless, and grasping for words to say, completely unprepared. Nobody wants to be in a situation like that. We have all experienced situations that create fear in our lives when there is no real threat or danger. This perceived threat disrupts our daily routines, strains relationships, limits our ability to work, and reduces self-esteem.

If you are dealing with this kind of fear, you are probably thinking about making mistakes all the time. It makes you avoid doing things because you would rather do nothing than do something and risk a mistake. This is called risk avoidance. This fear also obsesses a lot about mistakes you have already made in the past or imagines mistakes you could make in the future. It gets you coming and going! All these thoughts cause you to have overwhelming anxiety, which may make you feel panicky, nauseous, short of breath, dizzy, or experiencing a rapid heartbeat.

It can also lead to constant judgment and negative evaluation that you do not believe you are doing things perfectly, correctly or the right way. Some of the other symptoms of this kind of fear include indecisiveness, procrastination, constantly seeking reassurance and excessive checking of your work for mistakes. We all innately wish to be successful; however, on some level, we can at least anticipate and tolerate shortcomings and failed attempts when they happen. This fear will keep you feeling crushed by even the idea of a failed attempt. It will cause you to feel miserable and depressed. It is paralyzing and ultimately hinders you from stepping out, taking risks, and pursuing your goals and aspirations.

This fear causes you to set unrealistically high standards and unattainable goals for yourself because anything less than that might feel unacceptable to you. You have to be perfect, and you have to be prepared for anything. It will also cause you to build walls between yourself and anyone who is even slightly critical of you. You may not even be able to tolerate any criticism at all, even if that feedback is given constructively. To you, those words feel like an attack because they point out that you are not perfect. You tend to be overly critical of yourself and judge yourself way too harshly for not being able to attain your goals. Then, you will find yourself feeling stressed out when you even think about situations where you may not be at your best. Then, once again, you end up remembering all your past mistakes. You repeatedly play your mistakes over and over in your head, which causes you to be upset and angry. This fear literally steals your present time from you by presenting your imperfect past and your uncertain future to you.

In short, the fear of not being prepared will stop you in your tracks. It will keep you from living the life that God intended for you to have. There is no freedom in fear, and there is no peace in constantly feeling unprepared.

The Danger of the Fear of Not Being Prepared is that it undermines your confidence and self-belief, causing you to underestimate your capabilities and potential. It perpetuates a cycle of self-doubt and self-sabotage. The fear of not being prepared can be crippling, leading to anxiety and stress in life.

When you fear you are not prepared, you may put off tasks and responsibilities, thinking you will never be ready. This procrastination often leads to missed opportunities and increased stress as deadlines approach. The constant worry about not being prepared can make you less effective in your daily lives, too. You may start second-guessing your decisions, which leads to hesitancy and indecision. All of this can lead to performance anxiety. This anxiety can hinder your ability to perform at your best, and ultimately lead to underachievement. This fear can also cause physical health issues. The chronic stress that comes from the fear of being unprepared can have a huge negative impact on your physical health. It can easily lead to sleep disturbances, headaches, and more severe conditions like hypertension.

If this kind of fear is not dealt with, it can also contribute to mental health problems such as anxiety disorders, depression, and obsessive-compulsive tendencies. The constant preoccupation with your own fears can strain your relationships with friends and family. You may become distant or irritable. The fear of being unprepared can also cause you to pass up on opportunities, such as promotions or personal growth experiences, because you feel like you are not ready. If allowed to continue, this fear can also creep over into your financial matters and result in poor financial decisions, including overspending, the accumulation of debt, and neglecting your investments. It will not only cost you your time, but it will also cost you money!

If you constantly worry about being unprepared, you may lack the resilience needed to adapt to unexpected challenges and setbacks in life. Constantly worrying consumes your valuable time and mental energy that could be better spent on productive tasks and self-improvement. This leads to self-limiting beliefs, preventing you from taking risks and pursuing your goals with confidence. You may never realize your true capabilities if you constantly doubt yourself.

To alleviate the fear of not being prepared, you may become a perfectionist, setting impossibly high standards for yourself and experiencing chronic stress in your pursuit of flawlessness. It is then only a small step to stagnation and regret. One of the biggest dangers of this fear is that it leads to the nagging feeling of "what if" or "if only." Remember how we talked about that lovely little game a few chapters ago? The best way to avoid the effects of this fear is to simply overcome it completely and not allow it any place in your life.

Here are some Scriptures to Consider:

- Philippians 4:13 "I can do all things through him who strengthens me."

- Joshua 1:9 "Have I not commanded you? Be strong and courageous. Do not be frightened, and do not be dismayed, for the LORD your God is with you wherever you go."

- 2 Timothy 1:7 "For God gave us a spirit not of fear but of power and love and self-control."

- Proverbs 3:5-6 "Trust in the LORD with all your heart, and do not lean on your own understanding. In all your ways acknowledge him, and he will make straight your paths."

Overcoming the Fear of Not Being Prepared

Here are some detailed strategies to help you overcome this fear:

First, begin to set realistic expectations for yourself. Go ahead and acknowledge that nobody can be fully prepared for every situation. Perfection is an unrealistic goal. Instead, set achievable, specific goals and recognize that making mistakes is a natural part of life and growth. This one simple step will help you to reduce the fear of not being prepared.

You can also take a little time to learn to manage your anxiety. It is okay to explore some relaxation techniques and stress management strategies. Even though I no longer spend my days walking in fear, I still enjoy listening to the sounds of a distant thunderstorm. I find that that sounds very relaxing to me. Sometimes, I play that kind of sound while I am meditating on the word of God or even writing. Personally, it has a very soothing effect on me. Try taking some deep breaths and spending some time in silence, simply reflecting on the goodness of God. This can help you cope with the anxiety associated with this fear. As you continue to grow in the Lord and get to know him better, you will be able to stay calm and focused in the face of uncertain times.

Shift your mindset from a fear of inadequacy to a desire for continuous learning. Prioritize learning times more than perfection. Look at challenges as opportunities to gain new skills and knowledge rather than as threats to your competence. Embrace a growth mindset, which will allow you to improve and adapt over time. You need to visualize yourself succeeding in these areas! If you take time to see yourself handling situations confidently and competently, you will be able to reduce anxiety and increase your self-assurance. The Bible says, "As a man thinks in his heart, so is he." You will ultimately become what you think about. If you constantly see yourself as unprepared and failing, that is the direction your life will go. But, on the other hand, if you can imagine being successful and having answers to the questions you face, you will also go in that direction. You get to choose!

---

*You will ultimately become
what you think about.*

Another consideration is to learn to face your fears gradually rather than all at once. Our minds and bodies were never designed to be slapped around by fear, and trying to tackle everything in the world that is coming against you all at the same time is a daunting task for anyone. Cut yourself some slack. Learn to gradually tackle fear rather than feeling the pressure to overcome everything in life all at once.

Remember that overcoming fear is a process that takes some time and effort. It is important to be patient with yourself and celebrate your successes, no matter how small they may seem. Replace negative self-talk with positive affirmations and declarations of faith. Speak empowering statements about your abilities, worth, and God's faithfulness. Place your trust in God's provision and guidance. Lean on His strength and seek His wisdom in all your endeavors. Trust that He will equip you for the tasks He has called you to.

Ultimately, overcoming the fear of not being ready requires action. Step out in faith, trusting that God is with you and will guide you. Embrace the journey knowing that God can use your willingness and obedience for His purposes.

24

Fear of Rejection

Well, here's a little something we have all experienced, and let's be honest, it is not the best feeling in the world. Ever had your brilliant idea shot down right in front of you? Or maybe you have had that sinking sensation when your awesome presentation gets dismissed before you're even halfway through it. And, oh boy, how about when you pop the question, and someone just walks away without a word? Yeah, nobody's a fan of rejection. Deep down, we all crave acceptance for who we are. Even if our idea was not the greatest, it still stings to have it flat-out rejected, especially in front of others. The fear of rejection carries with it a fear of being humiliated or embarrassed.

It is true that feeling rejected is like getting a punch in the gut, emotionally and physically. It is a total rollercoaster of emotions. You are suddenly hit with a wave of shame and self-consciousness. You might feel like you are under a spotlight, and your self-esteem takes a nosedive. This can be very overwhelming and may lead to a sense of helplessness or vulnerability. You might feel like everyone is scrutinizing your every move, appearance, or word. This self-consciousness can be paralyzing and make it difficult to act naturally.

I remember seeing an advertisement by a popular airline company. The advertisement showed someone who had done something very embarrassing in front of many people, and then the announcer's voice came on and said, "Wanna get away?" That is what rejection does to you. It makes you want to escape. You might want to run and hide, or you may feel the urge to remove yourself from the public eye immediately. Escaping seems like the only way to alleviate the discomfort. It causes you to become acutely aware of yourself and your perceived flaws or inadequacies.

The fear of rejection can paralyze you, preventing you from acting. When we are afraid of being rejected, we may hesitate to pursue our goals, make new connections, or express our true feelings. This inaction can lead to missed opportunities and unfulfilled potential.

The fear of rejection is like having your feet glued to the ground. It makes you hesitate, second-guess yourself, and basically avoid going after your dreams, making new connections, or even expressing your true feelings. The feelings of rejection can last long after the initial incident, too. It might replay in your mind, keeping the emotional discomfort alive for quite a while. The lingering effects can affect your self-esteem and make you more cautious in similar situations in the future. It is easy at this point to become very harsh and self-critical. You might even engage in negative self-talk, berating yourself for your perceived mistake or inadequacy. All of this, of course, only leads to more humiliation. It can get ugly! But one of the most distressing aspects of rejection is the sense of losing control over your own emotions and reactions. This feeling of vulnerability can be disempowering and distressing. Once you experience rejection enough in your life, the next phase of social isolation begins. From here, it is a downward spiral.

Can you see how one thing leads to another? Can you see that it is a step-by-step process that leads to a dark place? Once you begin to isolate socially, you have inadvertently also cut yourself off from the very help you need. Since you do not want to feel exposed or vulnerable, you tend to withdraw from others so that your weaknesses cannot be seen. You certainly would not ever want to put yourself in a situation again that would bring the same results, so the fear of a repeat experience begins to guide your life.

I remember the first few times that I ever spoke publicly. I was so nervous that my knees were knocking together, and I felt nauseous. I was just trying to preach a few messages, but I could hardly get my words out. It was not because I had not studied enough, I certainly had. It was not because I was afraid to speak in front of people, I was not. All my fear at that time basically came from feelings of inadequacy and rejection. I just was not sure if the people I was speaking to would accept me or what I was saying. I was so overly concerned about what they thought of me that I could not even be myself. Eventually, I understood that it was not even about me! I was not standing in front of a bunch of people trying to deliver a gospel message for my sake but for their sake. I was trying to help them. Once I learned to get the focus off myself and onto helping people, everything changed. I remember hearing the story of a famous motivational speaker who was preparing to speak one evening to a large crowd of people. Someone met him in the green room before he went out to speak that night, and they asked him what he was thinking about right before he went out to speak. They certainly thought that he would say something like, "I am just concentrating on my notes to make sure that I get everything right." They thought he might say something about "just trying to stay focused on what I am going to say tonight." But his response was far different. What he said was, "I am just thinking about the people and how I can help them tonight!" Wow! That is a completely different way of thinking about it. Imagine what it would be like if we were not so concerned about being rejected, but rather more focused on helping people.

It is important to remember that feeling rejected, embarrassed, or humiliated is a shared human experience. Everyone, at some point, encounters moments of embarrassment and the loneliness that often follows. If you can recognize and relate to this, it can help reduce the stigma and feelings of isolation that come with this fear.

The Danger of the Fear of Rejection is that it destabilizes our "need to belong." We all have a fundamental need to belong to a group. When we fear being rejected, this need becomes destabilized and the disconnection we feel adds to our emotional pain. Fearing rejection creates surges of anger and aggression, leads to self-limiting beliefs, and results in social withdrawal, leading to isolation and feelings of loneliness. All of this becomes a barrier to forming meaningful connections and experiencing the richness of relationships. The fear of rejection often leads to avoiding risks and playing it safe.

This fear causes you to hide your true self and conform to societal expectations or the perceived preferences of others. This prevents the expression of their unique gifts, passions, and perspectives. Basically, you end up living a fake life because you remain afraid that people will not like your true self, the real you. Authenticity falls by the wayside and is replaced by a giant façade that you call life. This kind of fear coerces you into living your life solely for the acceptance of other people. And if you think about it, there is no life in that at all.

> *This kind of fear coerces you into living your life solely for the acceptance of other people.*

The fear of rejection sends us on a mission to destroy our self-esteem. We may even respond to romantic rejections by finding fault in ourselves, counting all our inadequacies, kicking ourselves when we are already down, and smashing our self-esteem into a pulp. Most romantic rejections are a matter of poor fit and a lack of chemistry, incompatible lifestyles, wanting different things at different times, or other such issues. Blaming ourselves and attacking our self-worth only deepens the emotional pain we feel and makes it harder for us to recover.

Here are some Scriptures to Consider:

- Romans 8:31: "What then shall we say to these things? If God is for us, who can be against us?"

- Psalm 34:17-18 "When the righteous cry for help, the LORD hears and delivers them out of all their troubles.

The LORD is near to the brokenhearted and saves the crushed in spirit."

- Isaiah 41:10 "Fear not, for I am with you; be not dismayed, for I am your God; I will strengthen you, I will help you, I will uphold you with my righteous right hand."

- 1 Peter 5:7 "Casting all your anxieties on him, because he cares for you."

Overcoming the Fear of Rejection

To overcome the fear of rejection, consider that you may be reading too much into it. Keep in mind that most of the time, fear is not even based on reality. Your feelings of timidity are all coming in advance. There is rejection, and then there is the fear of rejection. We are talking about the fear part. If you have faced rejection in the past, you must realize that that is not your permanent future. Just because something negative has happened to you does not mean that it's going to happen again.

Building up self-confidence and self-worth can help you remember that God still loves you and has a great plan for your life. Sometimes it is best to focus on all the good God has already done for you rather than concentrating on the things you have not seen yet. Overcoming the fear of rejection is a choice. The Bible tells us over and over that we are to choose to "fear not." You might be facing a myriad of thoughts coming against you, but it doesn't mean that you let them overcome you. You certainly do not! Challenge these negative thoughts in your mind. When thoughts of rejection and fear come to your mind, run to the word of God. Learn to identify negative thoughts and beliefs about yourself that fuel the fear of rejection and replace them with positive thoughts and truths that are grounded in God's love and His word.

Recognize that vulnerability can be a strength instead of a weakness. If you can present your authentic self to others, genuine connections can be built on honesty and vulnerability. Go ahead and develop a healthy sense of self-worth as you identify yourself as a child of God. Remember that your value was not determined by the opinions and acceptance of other people but by God's unconditional love for you. Understand that you may need to make some changes in your life. If you are constantly hanging out with people who are negative and perpetuate this fear in your life, you might consider getting some new friends. Hang out with people who support you and encourage you. Surround yourself with people who are going in the right direction.

As with so many of the other fears that we have already discussed, it is a good idea to extend some grace and compassion to yourself. You are not at the end of your journey, but the beginning. There is a quote that says, "It's not the size of the dog in the fight, but rather the size of the fight in the dog that counts." It's time for your freedom to get stronger than your fear! Let go of self-judgment and embrace self-love.

Instead of obsessing over your fear of rejection, shift your focus to serving and uplifting others. Engage in acts of kindness and contribute to the well-being of those around you. Redirecting your attention outward helps diminish self-centered fears. Rejection is an opportunity for growth and learning. Instead of internalizing rejection as a reflection of your worth, reflect on the experience and attempt to understand any lessons or areas for improvement. Place your trust in God's plan for your life. Surrender your fear of rejection to Him and trust that He will guide your steps, opening doors where you are accepted and cherished. Go where you are celebrated! Ultimately, find your complete acceptance and security in God's unwavering love and acceptance. Seek His approval above all else and rest in the assurance that His acceptance outweighs any rejection from others.

25

Conquering Fear Once and For All

Let me just say at this point that fear is not going to win over you! You are equipped with the tools that you need to overcome fear once and for all. One additional thing that I believe is helpful is to understand that everything starts with a seed. You know what it's like to go to the park and see that gigantic oak tree, right? Well, that huge tree started as a tiny acorn. Everything we see around us starts as a seed. Maybe that seed was a literal seed. Maybe that seed was a thought or an idea that eventually turned into something much bigger. If you think about it, everything that you see every day starts with just a thought or an idea. The chair you are sitting in right now was just a thought in someone's mind a long time ago. They challenged themselves and built upon that seed thought until there was a plan in place and a design created. Maybe the original plans for that chair or sketched on a napkin at a restaurant somewhere. Then, eventually, that design was approved by some engineer, moved into a manufacturing facility, fabricated, taken to a store, purchased by you, and ultimately sitting beneath you right now.

But it all started with a seed thought. An idea. Something in the mind.

With that in mind, isn't it easy to understand that fear can also be a seed? If your enemy, the devil, is allowed to plant a seed of fear in your mind, that seed can grow up to be a mighty, dominant thing in your life. If, on the other hand, you are constantly planting the seed of God's Word in your mind, you will also reap a harvest of great things in your life. It all depends on the seed that is sown and cultivated.

I want to take a little time to really talk about how seeds work. Trust me, this will not be a waste of time. In fact, this one simple set of thoughts could very well turn your whole life around. It may seem that talking about fear and talking about seeds have absolutely nothing in common, but they do. Let us take a closer look.

In **Mark 4:26-28** it says, "And he said, "The kingdom of God is as if a man should scatter seed on the ground. He sleeps and rises night and day, and the seed sprouts and grows; he knows not how. The earth produces by itself, first the blade, then the ear, then the full grain in the ear."

This verse says that the soil produces crops all by itself, even without outside help or interference from man. God designed the earth to work with seeds in just this way. It is something that God set in motion, not man! Or you could say it this way, the idea of seed, time, and harvest is a principle found in God's Word. There is nothing you can do to stop it or change it, it is a principle or a "law" that has been set in motion, just like gravity. This principle did not start taking place in the book of Mark in the New Testament but was initiated all the way back in the first chapter of Genesis. Listen to what the Bible says in **Genesis 1:11,** "And God said, "Let the earth sprout vegetation, plants yielding seed, and fruit trees bearing fruit in which is their seed, each according to its kind, on the earth." And it was so." And in **Genesis 8:22,** it says, "While the earth remains, seedtime and harvest, cold and heat, summer and winter, day and night, shall not cease."

Now, the scripture back in the book of Mark said that man planted the seed, then he just went to bed, and when he got up the next day, the seed was sprouting and growing, and he doesn't even know how. Over the years, using science, we have figured out a lot of different ways to grow crops and to make seeds sprout, but there is still so much that we do not understand. We have learned how to enrich soils to get better plants, we have learned how to eliminate soil altogether using hydroponics, and we have even learned how to crossbreed plants so that we end up with seedless watermelons and seedless grapes. We have learned how to "genetically modify" fruits and vegetables. But just know this: anytime you tamper with a principle spelled in God's Word and you alter it to do something else, usually, you get another negative result. Many times, we don't even know about the negative results until many decades later.

So, there are five observations I want to make:

1. God Himself put into practice the principle that when seeds are planted, they will grow. There is nothing you can do about that. It is His process.

2. A seed must be sown to grow. An unsown seed has an unrealized harvest. The seed will not grow unless it is planted!

3. Seeds only reproduce after their own kind. The fruit that grows from seed will always be of the same kind as the seed.

4. After the seed is planted, there is some amount of time that goes by before you see the results or eat the fruit of it.

5. As long as the earth remains, this process will continue.

With those five points in mind, let me just say that seeds can take on many forms and can be good or bad. We really need to learn the difference. This starts becoming very important when you consider the power of seeds in the light of fear. Again, if we allow the seeds of fear to be planted in our minds, then we will end up with a dark future as a harvest. The seeds of fear can be planted by our words, our actions, or our thoughts . . . or the absence of our words, actions, or thoughts. Think about it! What you do and say and think has a powerful impact on your life and literally sets the course of growth for the seed that has been planted. The seeds of your words, actions, and thoughts are a direct example to those around you of what you believe in, support, love, hate, and tolerate. Your seeds locate you!

However, if we choose to continuously plant the Word of God in our hearts and in our minds as a good seed, we will get the results of a wonderful, bountiful, joyous, hopeful harvest! Once a seed is planted, it will continue to grow. Seeds only grow bigger.

The simple fact is that the harvest of fear that you are currently experiencing in your life is the direct result of either seeds that you have sown in the past, or seeds of fear that you have allowed to remain there. So, if you don't like the harvest that has grown, check out the seeds that have been sown!

Fear will reproduce more fear,
and hope will reproduce more hope.

You've got to watch what kind of seed you are planting. Seeds will make or break your life. If you knowingly, willingly, and purposefully plant negative seeds of fear in your life, don't be surprised when a terrible harvest comes *your way.* If you knowingly, willingly, and purposefully plant positive seeds of faith and love in your life, don't be surprised when a wonderful harvest comes *your way.*

The good news is that even though a small seed can grow into a huge tree, it is also most vulnerable and at its weakest state when it is in seed form. This is a very important point! That means that there is no better or easier time to take care of a bad seed than in the very beginning. At its infancy. A bad seed that has started to sprout can easily be plucked out and destroyed. But nourish it and let it grow for a while, and now you've got a real problem. It is up to us to "Nip It In The Bud!" That's the best time to nip it.

Frustration can also set in when you do not understand the germination time of the seeds that have been planted in your life. When you don't consider the dormant time of seeds. There is seed, there is time, and there is harvest. Things take time!

Once a good or bad seed is planted, there is always a period that goes by before the resulting harvest is seen breaking the surface and sprouting. Just when it does not look like that terrible seed you planted is going anywhere, it sprouts up at the exact wrong time! Just when you think you are in the clear from filling your mind with terrible things, just when it seems like there will be no result from your stupid behavior, just when it looks like nothing will happen . . . it all happens! Fear comes rushing back in from seemingly nowhere. Sound familiar? It happens to all of us! The bottom line is that when any kind of seed is planted, it will grow and produce more of that same kind of thing. Fear will reproduce more fear, and hope will reproduce more hope. You can start to see that some things need to be planted, and some things need to be pruned! Some seeds need to be watered, and some need to be weeded. The Holy Spirit helps us know whether to nip it or nourish it. Do you want it to grow, or do you want it to go? Good things grow up to be great things, and bad things grow up to be terrible things. We must learn to be patient while the good things grow but quick to take action on the bad.

I warn you that weeding your garden can be a messy business, but it is worth it. Have you ever seen those gardening bags that have a kneeling pad attached to them? That is because to get all the weeds out, sometimes you need to spend some serious time on your knees, and not everyone is willing to do that.

The devil always shows you the worst-case scenario about the good God wants to do in your life. He says if you serve God, you will miss out on the fun. He says if you become a missionary, God will send you to the worst place in Africa. He says if you become a minister of the Gospel, all your friends will leave, and you will be alone. But he also shows you the best-case scenario when it comes to sin and pleasure and enjoyment. God does the opposite of all that and shows you the best-case scenario about serving God and the blessings that will come in your life by obedience to Him. And He shows you plainly and tells you the truth about how sin and wrongdoing will affect you and bring negative things into your mind and your thinking.

One of the worst seeds that you can ever plant is the seed of fear. Fear will grow and dominate. One of the best seeds that you can ever plant is the seed of love. Because love will also grow up and dominate. Remember that scripture we looked at earlier? God's perfect love casts out all fear!

26

The Rahab Principle

There is a wonderful story in the Old Testament, in Joshua Chapter 2. This is the story of how Joshua sent two of his men into the city of Jericho to check out the land. After these two men arrived in the city, they ended up at the house of a woman named Rahab. About this time, the king of Jericho was warned that these men had come to his city and were checking everything out, and he was not too happy to have spies in his city. Suspecting what was about to happen, the king ended up sending his own men to Rahab's house to find them, but Rahab had hidden the men until they could escape the city. She made up some fake story about how the men must have escaped during the night. So, the king's men proceeded to chase after them to no avail since they were still hidden on the roof of her house. Rahab ultimately had a conversation with the men to let them know she had heard so much about what God had already done throughout the land. She was convinced that God was going to give this land to them and Joshua. In return for her generosity in hiding them, she also struck a deal with them. Since she had kept them from harm, she wanted them to keep her and her family safe from harm or death when they returned to take over the land. She knew a lot of people would die in the process, and she wanted to make sure her family was safe. So, they agreed and made the deal. Then she lowered the men by rope down the city wall so they could escape this time and return to Joshua. But when the men reached the ground, they looked back up at Rahab and said to her that the deal would only be good if she tied a scarlet-colored rope in her window when they returned to take the city. This would be the identifying factor that the deal was still on.

Here is what the Bible says in **Joshua 2:18-21,** "Behold, when we come into the land, you shall tie this scarlet cord in the window through which you let us down, and you shall gather into your house your father and mother, your brothers, and all your father's household. Then, if anyone goes out of the doors of your house into the street, his blood shall be on his own head, and we shall be guiltless. But if a hand is laid on anyone who is with you in the house, his blood shall be on our head. But if you tell this business of ours, then we shall be guiltless with respect to your oath that you have made us swear." And she said, 'According to your words, so be it.' Then she sent them away, and they departed. And she tied the scarlet cord in the window."

This is so fascinating to me. There is more to this story than you might first think. Remember, after she made a deal with the spies, she then lowered them down out of her window with a rope. Then she gave them some last-minute escape instructions. But every mission of attack must have a signal that everyone agrees upon, and the spies said, "When we come into the land, you shall tie this scarlet cord in the window . . ." You must understand that once these men left her to go back to Joshua, it was quite a journey and took a great deal of time. So, just how long was it before they came back into the land? I am glad you asked!

According to my rough calculations based on what scripture indicates over the next few chapters, it happened about like this:

Once the men left her, they were in the hills by Jericho for three days, then journeyed back to Joshua. That took three more days. Then the Bible says that Joshua rose early in the morning, and they all traveled for a few more days and finally came to the Jordan River. Then in chapter five, God instructed Joshua to make knives out of flint and circumcise the whole nation, and in verse eight, it says that they remained there until they were completely healed. I checked with a medical professional regarding this whole procedure. She specializes in circumcision recovery, and she said that with today's medicine, the recovery time would be about two and a half weeks or seventeen more days. All this journeying and camping, and healing ended up consuming about forty-two days in total. What I am trying to say is that Rahab had about forty-two days to comply with what these two men asked her to do to keep her end of the deal. She had forty-two days to prepare and get ready to tie that scarlet cord in the window to keep the deal active.

Here is the good part! Look at what the Bible says about how long it took Rahab to accomplish this. The answer is right here in Joshua 2:21, where it says, "And she said, "According to your words, so be it." Then she sent them away, and they departed. And she tied the scarlet cord in the window."

How long did she wait? She waited absolutely no time at all! She did it right away! Wow! As soon as I realized this and saw it scripture for myself, I immediately thought of these questions:

- How long will you wait to do what you know will really help you?

- How long will you wait to be free from fear and overthinking?

- How long will you wait to get back to being a good spouse or parent to your children?

- How long will you wait to save your marriage?

Wouldn't you do anything to help your marriage, to serve that beautiful lady that God brought to you, to honor that wonderful man God put in your life? Wouldn't you do anything to bless them, encourage them, help them, lift them up? Wouldn't you do anything to finally be free from the chains of fear that have bound you for far too long? Wouldn't you do anything to press in and defeat the overthinking mentality that has plagued you your whole life? When will you finally commit to tying your own scarlet cord in the window?

Don't wait any longer to step out and do what you know in your heart is right! Waste no time! Now, this might just be my crazy thinking, but I don't believe she lowered the spies thirty feet down to the ground and then raised them back up to get the scarlet cord they were talking about. I believe she already had in her possession the whole time the very thing that God used to turn her whole family around! And ultimately, we can read in Hebrews 11:31 that, "By faith, Rahab the harlot did not perish along with those who were disobedient, after she had welcomed the spies in peace."

It worked! She acted quickly on what she knew was right, and so can you!

27

Scriptures to Study

Here is a list of **50** scriptures from the Bible that pertain to overcoming fear. These verses emphasize God's promises, strength, and guidance in times of fear and anxiety. I strongly encourage you to read through this list when you are facing fear. Reading through these verses will change your life! The words contained within these verses of scripture are a lifeline of hope and will give you a solid perspective right when you need it the most. These words bring life to you and faith to overcome any fear.

1. **Isaiah 41:10** — "Fear not, for I am with you; be not dismayed, for I am your God; I will strengthen you, I will help you, I will uphold you with my righteous right hand."

2. **Psalm 27:1** — "The Lord is my light and my salvation; whom shall I fear? The Lord is the stronghold of my life; of whom shall I be afraid?"

3. **Joshua 1:9** — "Have I not commanded you? Be strong and courageous. Do not be frightened, and do not be dismayed, for the Lord your God is with you wherever you go."

4. **2 Timothy 1:7** — "For God gave us a spirit not of fear but of power and love and self-control."

5. **Psalm 34:4** — "I sought the Lord, and he answered me and delivered me from all my fears."

6. **Isaiah 43:1** — "But now thus says the Lord, he who created you, O Jacob, he who formed you, O Israel: 'Fear not, for I have redeemed you; I have called you by name, you are mine.'"

7. **Psalm 56:3-4** — "When I am afraid, I put my trust in you. In God, whose word I praise, in God I trust; I shall not be afraid. What can flesh do to me?"

8. **Psalm 94:19** — "When the cares of my heart are many, your consolations cheer my soul."

9. **Philippians 4:6-7** — "Do not be anxious about anything, but in everything by prayer and supplication with thanksgiving let your requests be made known to God. And the peace of God, which surpasses all understanding, will guard your hearts and your minds in Christ Jesus."

10. **Psalm 55:22** — "Cast your burden on the Lord, and he will sustain you; he will never permit the righteous to be moved."

11. **Isaiah 26:3** — "You keep him in perfect peace whose mind is stayed on you, because he trusts in you."

12. **Matthew 6:25-27** — "Therefore I tell you, do not be anxious about your life, what you will eat or what you will drink, nor about your body, what you will put on. Is not life more than food, and the body more than clothing? Look at the birds of the air: they neither sow nor reap nor gather into barns, and yet your heavenly Father feeds them. Are you not of more value than they?"

13. **Romans 8:38-39** — "For I am sure that neither death nor life, nor angels nor rulers, nor things present nor things to come, nor powers, nor height nor depth, nor anything else in all creation, will be able to separate us from the love of God in Christ Jesus our Lord."

14. **Deuteronomy 31:6** — "Be strong and courageous. Do not fear or be in dread of them, for it is the Lord your God who goes with you. He will not leave you or forsake you."

15. **Psalm 118:6** — "The Lord is on my side; I will not fear. What can man do to me?"

16. **John 14:27** — "Peace I leave with you; my peace I give to you. Not as the world gives do I give to you. Let not your hearts be troubled, neither let them be afraid."

17. **Psalm 46:1-2** — "God is our refuge and strength, a very present help in trouble. Therefore, we will not fear though the earth gives way, though the mountains be moved into the heart of the sea."

18. **Proverbs 3:24** — "If you lie down, you will not be afraid; when you lie down, your sleep will be sweet."

19. **Psalm 34:17** — "When the righteous cry for help, the Lord hears and delivers them out of all their troubles."

20. **Isaiah 41:13** — "For I, the Lord your God, hold your right hand; it is I who say to you, 'Fear not, I am the one who helps you.'"

21. **Psalm 112:7** — "He is not afraid of bad news; his heart is firm, trusting in the Lord."

22. **Matthew 10:29-31** — "Are not two sparrows sold for a penny? And not one of them will fall to the ground apart from your Father. But even the hairs of your head are all numbered. Fear not, therefore; you are of more value than many sparrows."

23. **Psalm 55:22** — "Cast your burden on the Lord, and he will sustain you; he will never permit the righteous to be moved."

24. **1 Peter 5:7** — "Casting all your anxieties on him, because he cares for you."

25. **Psalm 56:11** — "In God I trust; I shall not be afraid. What can man do to me?"

26. **Isaiah 35:4** — "Say to those who have an anxious heart, 'Be strong; fear not! Behold, your God will come with vengeance, with the recompense of God. He will come and save you.'"

27. **Romans 8:31** — "What then shall we say to these things? If God is for us, who can be against us?"

28. **Psalm 23:4** — "Even though I walk through the valley of the shadow of death, I will fear no evil, for you are with me; your rod and your staff, they comfort me."

29. **Psalm 27:3** — "Though an army encamp against me, my heart shall not fear; though war arise against me, yet I will be confident."

30. **Psalm 112:6-7** — "For the righteous will never be moved; he will be remembered forever. He is not afraid of bad news; his heart is firm, trusting in the Lord."

31. **Isaiah 54:14** — "In righteousness you shall be established; you shall be far from oppression, for you shall not fear; and from terror, for it shall not come near you."

32. **Psalm 31:24** — "Be strong, and let your heart take courage, all you who wait for the Lord!"

33. **Psalm 118:4** — "Let those who fear the Lord say, 'His steadfast love endures forever.'"

34. **Psalm 112:8** — "His heart is steady; he will not be afraid, until he looks in triumph on his adversaries."

35. **Isaiah 12:2** — "Behold, God is my salvation; I will trust, and will not be afraid; for the Lord God is my strength and my song, and he has become my salvation."

36. **Isaiah 35:3-4** — "Strengthen the weak hands and make firm the feeble knees. Say to those who have an anxious

heart, 'Be strong, fear not! Behold, your God will come with vengeance, with the recompense of God. He will come and save you.'"

37. **Matthew 6:31-33** — "Therefore do not be anxious, saying, 'What shall we eat?' or 'What shall we drink?' or 'What shall we wear?' For the Gentiles seek after all these things, and your heavenly Father knows that you need them all. But seek first the kingdom of God and his righteousness, and all these things will be added to you."

38. **Isaiah 54:17** — "No weapon that is fashioned against you shall succeed, and you shall confute every tongue that rises against you in judgment. This is the heritage of the servants of the Lord and their vindication from me, declares the Lord."

39. **Isaiah 51:7** — "Listen to me, you who know righteousness, the people in whose heart is my law; fear not the reproach of man, nor be dismayed at their reviling's."

40. **Psalm 139:7-10** — "Where shall I go from your Spirit? Or where shall I flee from your presence? If I ascend to heaven, you are there! If I make my bed in Sheol, you are there! If I take the wings of the morning and dwell in the uttermost parts of the sea, even there, your hand shall lead me, and your right hand shall hold me."

41. **Isaiah 40:29-31** — "He gives power to the faint, and to him who has no might he increases strength. Even youths shall faint and be weary, and young men shall fall exhausted, but they who wait for the Lord shall renew

their strength; they shall mount up with wings like eagles; they shall run and not be weary; they shall walk and not faint."

42. **Psalm 34:9** — "Oh, taste and see that the Lord is good! Blessed is the man who takes refuge in him!"

43. **Psalm 91:15** — "When he calls to me, I will answer him; I will be with him in trouble; I will rescue him and honor him."

44. **Psalm 34:17-18** — "When the righteous cry for help, the Lord hears and delivers them out of all their troubles. The Lord is near to the brokenhearted and saves the crushed in spirit."

45. **Psalm 32:7** — "You are a hiding place for me; you preserve me from trouble; you surround me with shouts of deliverance."

46. **Psalm 34:10** — "The young lions suffer want and hunger; but those who seek the Lord lack no good thing."

47. **Psalm 34:19** — "Many are the afflictions of the righteous, but the Lord delivers him out of them all."

48. **Psalm 121:1-2** — "I lift up my eyes to the hills. From where does my help come? My help comes from the Lord, who made heaven and earth."

49. **Psalm 138:7** — "Though I walk in the midst of trouble, you preserve my life; you stretch out your hand against the wrath of my enemies, and your right hand delivers me."

50. **Psalm 139:1-3** — "O Lord, you have searched me and known me! You know when I sit down and when I rise up; you discern my thoughts from afar. You search out my path and my lying down and are acquainted with all my ways."

I hope these scriptures bring comfort, strength, and encouragement as you overcome fear and trust in God's promises.

Conclusion

Escaping the clutches of fear requires intentionality, faith, and a willingness to confront and overcome our fears. By seeking God's truth, renewing our minds, and surrounding ourselves with support, we can experience true freedom from fear's grip. To conquer fear, we must first acknowledge its existence in our lives. We must face it head-on, shining a light on the shadows it casts and refusing to let it dictate our actions. Denial only strengthens fear's grip, but the truth sets us free.

By understanding our fears — their origins, triggers, and manifestations, we gain much-needed insights into their hold on us. We can examine the patterns of perpetual fear and uncover the beliefs and thought processes that keep us trapped. This awareness is the foundation upon which we build our freedom from fear. Each time we confront our fears, however small, we chip away at their power and expand our ability to move forward. It is okay to acknowledge that setbacks and challenges are inevitable, but we also need to refuse to let fear use them as weapons against us. Instead, choose to embrace failure as an opportunity for growth, allowing it to propel you forward rather than hold you back.

Another powerful weapon against fear is knowledge. As we equip ourselves with understanding, insights, resources, and personal experiences, we also become better prepared to deal with fear. The more prepared we are, the more we learn to prioritize rest and engage in activities that bring us joy. By investing in ourselves, we replenish our reserves and build resilience to face fear head-on.

Make no mistake; fear can be deeply ingrained and conquering it does require patience and understanding. Once we openly acknowledge that setbacks and moments of vulnerability are part of the process, we are then free to treat ourselves with kindness and grace, celebrating every small victory along the way.

The path toward conquering fear leads to a profound transformation taking place within us. In our minds and in our hearts. Fear's grip loosens, and a new freedom emerges. We step into a life where fear no longer dictates and dominates our choices.

So, a summary of steps to conquer fear could look like this:

1. Face the fact that fear is real and terrible.

2. Acknowledge that fear is not from God, and He is not your enemy.

3. Understand that fear is a deception that takes place in your mind.

4. Know that you do not have to accept fear.

5. Recognize that you have a choice in the matter.

6. Learn to "let not" your heart be troubled.

7. Continue to fill your mind with God's Word.

8. Accept God's wonderful, supernatural peace in your heart and mind.

9. Conclude that you will keep moving through life.

10. Choose to start today, not tomorrow.

Take these principles to heart and determine to change. Be gentle with yourself because conquering fear is a process. And while the journey may have its challenges, know that God is with you every step of the way, empowering you to live a life marked by courage, faith, and unwavering trust in Him. I sincerely hope that you embark on this journey with hope, knowing that freedom from fear is within your reach.

So, fear, beware! It is time to unleash the power within, rely on God's strength, and embrace the journey toward fearless living. Remember that fear's power is limited. It may have haunted you for far too long, but you possess the power, with Gods help, to turn things around for good! Embrace the wonderful journey called life and claim your victory right now. It is time to **Go Live Life!**

Receive Jesus as Your Savior

Choosing to receive Jesus Christ as your Lord and Savior is the most important decision you will ever make!

God's Word promises in Romans 10:9, 10, & 13, "If you confess with your mouth that Jesus is Lord and believe in your heart that God raised him from the dead, you will be saved. For with the heart, one believes and is justified, and with the mouth, one confesses and is saved. For everyone who calls on the name of the Lord will be saved."

By His grace, God has already done everything to provide salvation for you. Your part is simply to believe and receive what Jesus has already provided.

Pray this out loud, and really mean it from your heart:

Jesus, I confess that You are my Lord and Savior. I believe in my heart that God raised You from the dead. By faith in Your Word, I receive salvation now. Thank You for saving me!

The very moment you commit your life to Jesus Christ, the truth of His Word instantly comes to pass in your spirit. Now that you're born again, there is a brand-new you!

Receive the Holy Spirit

As His child, your loving heavenly Father wants to give you the supernatural power you need to live this new life.

The Bible says in Luke 11:10,13, "For everyone who asks receives, and the one who seeks finds, and to the one who knocks it will be opened. If you then, who are evil, know how to give good gifts to your children, how much more will the heavenly Father give the Holy Spirit to those who ask him!"

All you do is ask, believe, and receive!

Pray, Father, I recognize my need for Your power to live this new life. Please fill me with Your Holy Spirit. By faith, I receive it right now! Thank You for baptizing me. Holy Spirit, You are welcome in my life.

Congratulations! Now you're filled with God's supernatural power. Some syllables from a language you don't recognize will rise from your heart to your mouth. (Check out 1 Corinthians 14:14 for more details) As you speak those words out loud by faith, you are releasing God's power from within and building yourself up in the spirit. You can do this whenever and wherever you like.

It doesn't really matter whether you felt anything or not when you prayed to receive the Lord and His Spirit. If you believed in your heart that you received, then God's Word promises you did. The Bible says in Mark 11:24, "Therefore I tell you, whatever you ask in prayer, believe that you have received it, and it will be yours." God always honors His Word; believe it!

If you have prayed to receive Jesus as your Savior or to be filled with the Holy Spirit, I congratulate you and rejoice with you. Welcome to your new life in Christ!

Additional Resources

Listed below are some references I used while doing my study on fear and its effects. If you wish to do additional study on the topic I suggest you look at these resources.

- Impact of Fear and Anxiety — University of Minnesota Earl E. Bakken Center for Spirituality & Healing https://www.takingcharge.csh.umn.edu/impact-fear-and-anxiety Fear can interrupt processes in, intense emotions and impulsive reactions.

- How to Remove Fear & Get Strength – Life Is a Journey, part 17 by Pastor Richard Rogers: https://agfaithchapel.org/sermons-messages/how-to-remove-fear-and-get-strength-life-is-a-journey-part-17

- https://www.healthline.com/health/mental-health/time-anxiety#managing-it

- Fear of public speaking: https://hbr.org/2019/09/to-overcome-your-fear-of-public-speaking-stop-thinking-about-yourself